TANGO FOR BEGINNERS

A GUIDE TO USING SHARED GOVERNANCE TO WORK THROUGH THE TWISTS AND TURNS OF HIGHER-EDUCATION RELATIONSHIPS

———————

SUSAN C. TURELL, PH.D.
MARIA THOMPSON, PH.D.

———————

ACADEMIC IMPRESSIONS | 2024
DENVER, CO

Published by Academic Impressions.

CR Mrig Company. 5299 DTC Blvd., Ste. 1400. Greenwood Village, CO 80111.

Cover design by Brady Stanton.

For reproduction, distribution, or copy permissions, or to order additional copies, please contact the Academic Impressions office at 720.488.6800 or visit:

www.academicimpressions.com

Academic Impressions

ISBN 978-1-948658-24-9

Printed in the United States of America.

MORE FROM THESE AUTHORS

Courageous Gardening: Equity-Minded Leadership in Higher Education

Can our environment, our institutions, be a landscape in which every living being thrives? Can we create the best possible soil to nourish all, to allow the potential within each of us to flourish? We believe the answer is yes. Get *Courageous Gardening* here:

https://www.academicimpressions.com/product/equity-minded-leadership-higher-education/

"Turell and Thompson have captured the essence of how to engage and enact transformational change focusing on equity and inclusion. Their garden metaphor encourages both self and institutional reflection, essential components to authentic systemic transformation." – *Sue Rankin, President, Rankin Climate*

"In this compelling and well-conceptualized workbook, Dr. Turell and Dr. Thompson aptly use the metaphor of gardening, relating principles and skills utilized by a master gardener to guide the reader through a parallel process of self-exploration, intersectional realities, and the overall complex and nuanced landscape of DEI in higher education. For those looking for a practical roadmap on how to make meaningful and sustainable systemic change in the DEI space at their institutions, *Courageous Gardening Equity-Minded Leadership in Higher Education* is a must-read." – *Carlos N. Medina, Vice President, Senior Consultant, and Practice Lead for Diversity and Inclusion, Academic Search*

"*Courageous Gardening* is a masterpiece because it thoughtfully and methodically explains what it means to be an equity-minded leader, and because it provides case studies and activities so that the reader is actively engaged in the process of understanding how to, what to, and why. The workbook facilitates application and provides the reader with an opportunity to critically examine their own landscape, and to work to create cultivating change or a new landscape. This is required reading, especially chapters 5 and 10—which once read, you will find yourself referring back to again and again. Highly recommend: 5 stars." – *Usheevii King, Assistant Vice Provost, Faculty Engagement and Development, New York University*

SUSAN C. TURELL AND MARIA THOMPSON

REVIEWS

"In *Tango for Beginners*, Turell and Thompson use the apt analogy of a complex dance to elucidate the challenges of shared governance. The framing of the challenge is especially sharp, as it honors the roles of both leaders and followers, in contrast to many works that focus on the leader only. The work reflects a rich understanding of multiple campus constituencies and addresses each aspect of potential conflict from each perspective. Turell and Thompson bring insights from their extensive interviews with multiple groups, making the book appropriate for most higher-education audiences. The reflection exercises encourage the reader to note defensive or territorial behaviors, to question assumptions of dishonesty or ill intentions, and to keep the purpose—educating students – at the center of all discussions. They also call attention to hierarchy and privilege, challenging us to ensure that those who stay quiet are given voice and to avoid letting louder individuals dominate or speak for others. The book concludes with a series of case studies and reflection questions that allow readers to practice their newfound insights and work through some common scenarios that bring shared governance into focus. I highly recommend this resource to all with a commitment to shared governance, shared purpose, and a desire to reach better decisions through inclusive processes." — Sara L. Zeigler, Professor of Political Science, Provost and Senior Vice President for Academic Affairs, Eastern Kentucky University

"This book will be very helpful to college and university leaders who want to gain a better understanding of the meaning and role of shared governance in higher education. The authors' masterful use of dance as a metaphor is an effective approach to illustrating the importance of shared governance in leading an institution. The case studies will be especially helpful to the reader in stimulating productive discussions about critical aspects of leadership."—Freeman A. Hrabowski, III, President Emeritus, UMBC

"*Tango for Beginners* captures the importance of trust, communication, and understanding the role each of us plays to effectively develop, sustain, and ultimately use shared governance in the increasingly complex landscape of higher education. Dr. Turell and Dr. Thompson have written a useful and timely workbook for beginners as well as a reminder for experienced academics of the importance of collaboration, transparency, and data-informed strategy setting within our institutions… The case studies provide an engaging opportunity to distance oneself from a current setting and perhaps recognize ourselves and our situations in a new light to work for the common good." — Mary Strey, VPAA and Dean of Faculty, Central College

"In *Tango for Beginners*, Turell and Thompson offer a powerful and fascinating guide to engaging higher education's most complex issue: shared governance. So aptly titled, the book is about the communication and relationship dance in the life of the academy by all stakeholders, which is so necessary to advance institutional mission and strategic priorities. [Readers are addressed] in a language that is thoughtful and insightful and that resonates with our common experiences as learners, teachers, scholars, advocates, activists, and administrators. *Shared governance is not the enemy. Shared governance is a friend when managed well. …Tango for Beginners* is a must-read for all of us in higher education who are deeply committed to the service of our institutions and the public good." —Peter O. Nwosu, Ph.D. Professor of Communication Studies and President, State University of New York (SUNY) at Oswego, New York

CONTENTS

"Life's a dance you learn as you go.
Sometimes you lead, sometimes you follow."

—John Michael Montgomery, *"Life's a Dance"*

PREFACE

Why This Workbook

Shared. Governance. Use these two words separately, and there tends to be agreement regarding their meaning. Use these two words together in the context of higher education in the United States and Canada, and agreement on the meaning of this phrase is significantly less. A brief perusal of higher education trade publications will make it clear that differing interpretations of shared governance are at the root of numerous disagreements among campus stakeholder groups. The result of these disagreements often leads to votes of no confidence, abrupt resignations, endless disputes about who makes what decisions, issues—big and small—that never seem to get resolved, and a general feeling of dissatisfaction with the working relationships among campus constituencies.

We interviewed presidents/chancellors; provosts; faculty senate, staff senate, and student government leaders; and board members at higher education institutions across the spectrum—public and private institutions, four-year and two-year institutions, research and regional comprehensive universities, and HBCUs, HSIs, and PWIs—to get a sense of some of the pain points and understand the efforts to resolve both recurring and emerging issues:

- Recurring issues tend to center on transparency, authority, and process. At the root of these issues is the unexamined and unprocessed history of campus conflicts that have led to intransigence and distrust, resulting in verbal attacks, disengagement, and passive-aggressive "gotchas."

- New or emerging issues—many caused by the disruption of the COVID-19 pandemic, changing demographics, and polarizing politics at the national, state, and local levels—were reported to be met with blocking and stall tactics, a refusal to engage in shared governance, verbal attacks, and leaks of confidential information via social, news media, and the good old campus grapevine.

These common responses to working with the "opposition" are not strengthening our institutions. However, it is possible and necessary to create a healthier shared governance on campuses. We recommend that a place to start is to replace these tactics with a combination of productive questioning and the challenging of long-held assumptions (discussed further in Chapter One).

But first, if shared governance is to *work*, we need a new, shared understanding of what shared governance is, and *how* it is to work. And it *can* work—if we approach it not as a duel but as a dance. We hope you enjoy the steps we lay out, as you consider a fresh approach to shared governance.

The Dance of Human Interaction

Human interactions are often referred to as a dance—a form of nonverbal communication through movement of the body. Dance involves more than *just* movement. Moving one's body, after all, can be almost involuntary, a result of the natural impulses and instincts of corporal existence. Examples of such instinctive movement include swatting away a fly, scratching an itch, or reaching reflexively to catch a falling object. So, what distinguishes dance from these ordinary movements? What raises it to the level of an art form? The answer is *intention*—the intentional practice of a skill that leads to the intentional expression of human moods and emotions. To perform a dance, the dancer "requires unaccustomed patterns of muscular exertion and relaxation as well as an unusually intense or sustained expenditure of energy."[1]

In the dance that takes place among constituency groups on college campuses, certain routines have become like natural impulse, nearly instinctive. That is what has occurred with the unproductive responses to recurring and emerging issues we listed on the previous page. To move out of these ruts, all parties must abandon old, unproductive patterns of relating and replace them with different ways of interacting.

The aim of this workbook is to guide campuses as they explore "unaccustomed patterns of muscular exertion and relaxation and the unusually intense or sustained expenditure of energy" needed to create healthy, productive shared governance.

With consistent, intentional practice, constituency groups can collectively build new musculature and sufficient stamina to navigate shared governance challenges with skill and grace.

Shared Governance as Tango

Drama. Passion. Drops. Kicks. Twirls. Slow movements. Quick movements. Sudden changes in direction. These words can be used to describe both the Tango and shared governance. When well executed, both the Tango and shared governance demonstrate the power of partnership and its ability to create a functional, cohesive whole from separate parties. When poorly executed, dysfunctional, arrhythmic outcomes can be the result—the consequence of failed communication and a lack of synchronized effort.

We use the analogy of the Tango throughout this workbook to illustrate the dynamic, complex nature of separate parties working together to create a cohesive, functioning whole. The breathtaking beauty of the Tango is created by each dancer executing different dance moves simultaneously. Like shared governance, the Tango consists of those who lead and those who follow. There is beauty and skill involved in both leading and following, and each dancer depends on the other. Neither role is considered better than the other. The same holds for shared governance. There are those who lead and those who follow. The role that each party plays differs, and each role requires thoughtfulness and skill to help the university thrive. Neither role is considered better than the other— leaders and followers have different functions and equal humanity.

---

[1] Mackrell, Judith R. "Dance." *Encyclopaedia Britannica*. October 18, 2023, https://www.britannica.com/art/dance.

How to Use This Workbook

This workbook is designed to be used by some or all constituency groups working together to strengthen shared governance at a college or university. The perfect time to use the information in this book is now, whether there has been a change in leadership (which is happening with increasing frequency), and/or an influx of new faculty and staff, or whether the same teams have been in place for a long time. The information can be used at major transition points and over time to renew constituency groups' commitment to working together for the common good.

We have designed this workbook as a practical tutorial, comprising two parts: **The Dance Steps** and **Case Studies**. You will also find an activity (writing an effective charge) in the Appendix.

Part 1: The Dance Steps

Each chapter contains what we refer to as *dance steps* to be learned. These dance steps present you with the information that each constituency group should consider regarding various aspects of shared governance as it applies to their role. As you read the dance steps, consider them an opportunity to rehearse ideas and practices. Rehearsing outside of actual shared governance processes may help to implement them during higher-stakes situations.

Each chapter will begin with a narrative contextualizing these steps; then, at the end of each section or chapter, we will provide the steps, which are specific ideas for navigating the dance of shared governance (both *intrapersonal* and introspective steps to take, and *interpersonal* steps to take), with a list for each constituency (administrators, faculty, staff, board of trustees, and students). These are the dance steps you need to learn to fulfill your role in the Tango effectively. You will note that some of these steps are unique to a specific constituency, while others apply to all.

Following the dance steps, at the end of each section or chapter, we will also include several pages of Self-Reflection questions for all readers. These are intended to help you to explore and think more deeply about the ideas in each chapter. You may wish to answer some for yourself; others might work better as a catalyst for discussion among various members of shared governance groups, either within or across constituencies.

Taken together, the seven chapters of this book provide a practical rehearsal in the essential 'dance steps' for the Tango of shared governance. This 'dance steps' tutorial consists of the following topics:

CHAPTER ONE

This chapter explores *leading* and *following* within the context of shared governance, as well as the role of assumptions in helping or hindering effective shared governance. Central to this discussion is the understanding and delineation of the roles of each party in various situations. It is necessary to have a common definition of shared governance as a starting point, but this alone is not sufficient. Each constituent group may bring their own assumptions about the purpose and processes for shared governance, which can lead to a quagmire in which parties work at cross purposes. In this chapter, we will first offer some general observations that apply across constituent groups, and then we will examine possible assumptions that might be commonly held by each party. The first chapter concludes with a trust matrix which is designed to help increase the level of trust among and between constituency groups.

CHAPTER TWO

Sphere of influence and power dynamics are the focal points of our second chapter. We ask you to consider your roles, both formal and informal, and to examine the power you have to influence others. We also discuss the ability to influence others based on both visible and invisible identities. For any given shared governance policy and practice, your voice will be heard differently by those who share your identity than it will by those who do not. Further, your voice will be heard differently based on your intersecting identities. Lastly, we encourage you to use your sphere of influence with intentionality and to examine your approach to power/control, as well as the role that power dynamics play in the process.

CHAPTER THREE

Our third chapter delves into the structural issues related to shared governance, exploring such topics as the different types of organizational structures and 'elected' vs. 'selected' membership. The impact of administrators attending faculty and staff senate meetings as ex-officio or with voting rights is also discussed. The final topic of this chapter is consultation. What counts as consultation? When and how should formal and informal structures be used for consultation?

CHAPTER FOUR

Strategic vs. operational outcomes are the topic of this chapter. Shared governance most often calls to mind the development and review of operational policies or practices, but it also plays an important role in planning the strategic direction of an institution. Shared governance processes can also play a vital role in creating meaningful paradigm shifts in mission, vision, or values. Disagreement and resistance is expected and necessary when potential new directions for the institution are on the table. In such times, shared governance processes can be used to successfully manage opposing views while moving the campus toward new ways of being and toward strategic thinking.

CHAPTER FIVE

Central to the success of shared governance is communication, which is the focus of the fifth chapter. Chapter One initially discussed the definition of shared governance; Chapter Five returns to it, as this definition is one of the cornerstones of successful shared governance. We discuss the need for two levels of communication—*within* groups and *among* groups. We also discuss the importance of sharing data broadly to ensure transparency, because communication among constituencies is often challenged by the concept of transparency and how it is defined.

CHAPTER SIX

Shared governance also requires finding the 'right' tempo and timing, which is the focus of Chapter Six. The processes must allow adequate time for articulating the purpose and task at hand, gathering data (including consultation), and producing a timeline for a decision and implementation. "Adequate," however, might have different meanings for different constituencies and about different issues. We explore the potential benefits and pitfalls of constituency groups manipulating the tempo of shared governance for perceived advantage. We also discuss the impact of semester/quarter boundaries on the tempo of shared governance.

CHAPTER SEVEN

The seventh chapter concludes the tutorial by encouraging campuses to engage in the creation of a *shared governance roles and responsibilities matrix* so that constituency groups can clarify the "who does what, when" question. We also have suggestions for campuses who may find the matrixed approach overly structured and restrictive. Lastly, we discuss the often-neglected topic of the evaluation and continuous improvement of shared governance. We recommend instituting formal evaluations, such as surveys, to be administered at regular intervals, involving all stakeholder groups. Less formal and more frequent means of assessing shared governance are recommended as self-assessments—a way for constituency groups to take responsibility for their own roles in healthy or unhealthy shared governance.

Part 2: Case Studies

Once you have completed your rehearsal, it's time to get out on the dance floor and practice what you have learned. The **case studies** found at the end of this book will help you to hone your insight and perspective on shared governance, and will help you and your colleagues discuss strategies and ideas for improvement. The case studies follow the work lives of the faculty, staff, students, and administrators of the fictional Jackson Rockgrove University. You can explore the mission and values, org chart, and cast of characters at JRU on pages 95-98.

You may decide to engage with this workbook as an individual, in a group of peers, or in a group composed of representation across constituencies. An inter-constituency group may yield the most applied progress. In any formulation, responses to the case studies and activities can be shared between and among groups to gain insights into:

1) Each other's perspectives.
2) What strategies and tactics are working to create productive shared governance.
3) What needs improvement.

As with our other workbooks, matters of diversity, equity, and inclusion are embedded throughout the book. We hope that as you use this workbook and engage with its ideas and activities, you will find ways to improve how shared governance works at your institution so that all constituencies feel that they are partners in its dance.

PART ONE:
THE DANCE STEPS

CHAPTER ONE: STEPS AND MISSTEPS— SHARED GOVERNANCE ROLES AND ASSUMPTIONS

"If you are searching for keys and you assume that the keychain is green, your mind will ignore everything except green."—Shunya

---

TOPICS COVERED IN THIS CHAPTER:

- Leading and following within the context of shared governance

- Assumptions and their role in helping or hindering effective shared governance

- Building trust within and across constituency groups

Learning the Tango: The Roles of Leader and Follower

The Tango is designed to bring people together—as is shared governance.

One reason the Tango is such a good metaphor for shared governance is the importance it places on the capacity inherent to every role. Both the leader and the follower in the Tango have a role in creating the dance. Each role is separate and equally significant. The leader communicates the patterns of the dance through decisions about movement. While it might look like the leader has control, the leader is also taking cues from the follower to help guide the steps and create the entire dance. The follower is sensitive to the signals of the leader and responds accordingly. Both dancers collaborate on the choreography before the dance is formally executed.

Within shared governance, the leader is the one who has authority to make something happen. The authority might rest with the person who has responsibility for the budget. It might rest with the person who can be fired if the initiative doesn't result in the required measurable outcomes. In these cases, the leader will likely be an administrator. Per the American Association of University Professors (AAUP), faculty are in the leadership role for curriculum and personnel processes related to tenure and promotion.

In all cases, collaboration is key.
Regardless of who is in the leader role, control over the partner is not the goal:
empowerment to fulfill the institutional mission is the goal.

To add to the complexity, the followers might be faculty, staff, students, or administrators. The leader may be a board of trustees, administrators, or faculty; sometimes the leader role is delegated. Throughout this book, we refer to each group as a constituency, since its members are situated similarly at the university. Although individual members may have different experiences, their shared relationship to the university often creates a worldview about the institution and its shared governance.

Probably the biggest challenge facing shared governance is when each constituency brings a definition of shared governance that differs from each other's. Until and unless a shared definition is articulated, the process will remain disjointed and unnecessarily difficult.

Having a common definition of shared governance lets everyone know that you are dancing a Tango, rather than a waltz, hip-hop, or two-step. Yet having a common definition as a starting point is not enough, as each constituent group may bring their own assumptions about the purpose and processes for shared governance. These assumptions, if left hidden and unspoken, can also trip us up. Rather than dancing together, assumptions can lead us to unintentionally stepping on toes.

In this chapter, we first offer some observations about *common assumptions* regarding shared governance. Then, we address how to build *trust*, which underpins the process for creating shared assumptions and the definitions for shared governance.

To use shared governance more effectively, and to join each other across differences, each constituency should keep a focus on:

- Student learning as the mission of all of higher education.

- The unique mission, vision, and values of your institution.

- The understood and agreed-upon definitions of *shared governance* and *consultation* at your institution.

With that in mind, let's take a closer look at the most common assumptions that can trip us up:

Assumption #1: Shared governance is adversarial

The most common assumption in higher education is that faculty, staff, and administrators are natural adversaries; this leads to the assumption that *shared governance is adversarial*. As we listened to people discuss shared governance, they almost always used 'us vs. them' language, as though these adversarial relationships are a given. We often hear people speak of 'the other side,' as if there are two sides.

Yet, if we approach shared governance as a choreographed Tango, does it make sense to assume that our partner will try to trip us? What stops us from assuming good intentions, even though we are in different roles? How might we help to challenge this assumption of adversarial motives, and at least hold the possibility that we can—and want to—work together across differences?

Assumption #2: Shared governance means shared decision making

Another assumption is that *shared governance means shared decision making*. This assumption is misleading and ignores the reality that not all constituents are responsible for the effects of each decision. It helps to keep in mind that those who are authorized to make the decision are also those who are accountable for its outcomes.

For example, decisions that have a large financial impact on overall institutional health mostly fall to those in administration. They are held responsible for the current and future financial viability of the institution. While other constituents should rightly have input, they are not the institutional officers accountable for the revenue and expenses and for the institution to be solvent.

In another example, personnel decisions about promotion and tenure are typically made by faculty, both within the discipline and institution-wide. Faculty committees are responsible for ensuring that their faculty colleagues are educating students with the foundational and current knowledge and skills within their discipline. They are also responsible for ensuring that their colleagues are meeting the job requirements of teaching, research, and service, as applicable. While there is administrative oversight, this oversight typically should not be used to override faculty decisions unless there are compelling reasons to do so (reasons sometimes unknown to faculty colleagues due to confidentiality policies).

In each of these examples, neither constituent should be responsible for the other's purview. To assume such responsibility implies a lack of respect for the intentions and abilities of other constituencies. This assumption often occurs when the role of consultation is misunderstood.

Assumption #3: Consultation is equal to shared decision making

A third faulty assumption is that *consultation is equal to shared decision making*. It's imperative that each institution have a solid understanding of consultation, as we discuss in Chapter Two. Sometimes we provide input, and the decision does not align with that input. When this happens, for effective shared governance we suggest you consider substituting a more optimistic assumption that the decision makers have a broader or deeper (or both broader *and* deeper) understanding of the issues, and that the decision is being made in that broader, deeper context, including our input. Sometimes there are conflicting and compelling matters that need to be weighed, and there is a better solution than what we proposed, though not a perfect one.

To manage expectations and assumptions, all parties may wish to consider the following. If each constituent follows these, doing so may minimize missteps:

- Be skeptical of one's knowledge, and approach the process with a mindset of learning more about what others think about a situation. While each constituent knows important information from their vantage point and role, consider that few if any have a complete view. Consultation helps to fill in missing gaps for those who need to make the decision and can lead to organizational learning about issues important to the campus.

- Be clear about which decisions fall to your constituency. If the decision is yours to make, be sure to consult. There is a lot of heterogeneity within each constituency; consultation may need to be both within and across constituency group members.

- Be clear about each issue and decision to be made. Is it shared governance, shared decision making, and/or shared responsibility? Each may be operating, or these may overlap. The more these can be discerned, the more you can question assumptions, and engage with more clarity.

The Dance Steps

As we mentioned in the preface, at the end of each section or chapter in this book, we will provide "Dance Steps" to be learned, so that you can fulfill your role in the Tango of shared governance more effectively. These are specific ideas for navigating the dance of shared governance (both *intra*personal and introspective steps to take, and *inter*personal steps to take), with a list for each constituency (administrators, faculty, staff, board of trustees, and students). You will note that some of these steps are unique to a specific constituency, while others apply to all.

Following the Dance Steps, each chapter also includes several pages of Self-Reflection questions for all readers. These are intended to help you to explore and think more deeply about the ideas in each chapter.

This first chapter will be unique in that it will present two sets of Dance Steps. These steps consist of understanding what each constituency needs to know about shared governance in relation to challenging one's assumptions (on pages 15-18) and building trust (on pages 22-27). Together, these two sets will help you both lead or follow well, whichever is needed.

As you read these, note that you can use these steps in your current role and *also* to help understand the perspectives of others with whom you are working to create effective shared governance.

What each constituency needs to know about shared governance in relation to assumptions

As you identify assumptions during your shared governance processes—both your own assumptions and others'—making these explicit can help to examine them. If these assumptions are operating, they are important to note so that they can be questioned if they are inaccurate—or, if accurate, embedded into the process.

DANCE STEPS: ASSUMPTIONS
Intrapersonal • Be sure you have a clear idea of which decisions are yours and which rightly belong to others. • Try to listen for and challenge an "us vs. them" mentality, both for yourself and others. • Find common ground around mission and values.
Interpersonal • Sometimes decisions made by others have financial impacts that fall under your purview. Be sure to provide transparent financial information, even in an overview or in the aggregate. • When creating a process and/or the charge for the work to be done, provide an outside frame for shared governance work (e.g., the Boyer model). This will provide needed information and context to any 'charge' provided. • When creating a process and/or the charge for the work to be done, by role, be clear about whose decision it is and who is being consulted. • Part of the job of an administrator is to bring people together. Decide whose voices need to be part of the processes of consultation, information gathering, and decision making. The constituencies most affected need to be included. • Framing a new initiative as a pilot is both truthful and useful. Higher education needs innovation. You need to advocate to try new methods and new initiatives; at the same time, you need to be willing to admit when they need to be stopped or significantly modified.
Intrapersonal • Be sure you have a clear idea of which decisions are yours and which rightly belong to others. • Try to listen for and challenge an "us vs. them" mentality, both for yourself and others. • Find common ground around mission and values.

The left edge of the table is labeled vertically: **ADMINISTRATORS**

- You are an expert in your discipline, but not an expert about higher education. Own that. Ask questions and get the information you need to make good decisions in areas that involve shared governance outside your disciplinary scope.

- Sometimes, it really IS the decision of the Board of Trustees or administration. In those cases, use your consultation role to provide the information they need to make a better decision.

- Check if your default assumption is to prefer to maintain the status quo. The assumption that the 'way we always did it' is better is often not true, given the rapid societal changes and generational changes.

- Sometimes it's hard to let go of perfection when shared governance results in new ideas, initiatives, or projects. Consider new initiatives as pilot projects that can be imperfect, evaluated, tweaked, or discarded.

Interpersonal

- There are times that faculty are not told every detail or provided with confidential information, and the default assumption can be that you are not trusted. While that can be true, more often it is due to other reasons. A few to consider are:

    ○ They don't know that you don't know. (Always ask for what you want to know.)

    ○ The data is confidential, such as many personnel matters. (Accept this. You wouldn't want others to know your confidential information.)

    ○ The details are not as relevant to the decision as you suspect. (And can be overwhelming to digest, or not worth the time to digest them.)

    ○ They don't have the data. (Sometimes it's hard to get or not possible to gather.)

    ○ Other faculty have been untrustworthy in the past and they are painting you with the same brush. (Someone once mentioned that holding something in confidence meant 'telling only one person.' Seriously, if burned in the past, many will assume it of most/all others. See our workbook *Running the Race* for more about building trust.)

- Tied to the assumption above, you have the right to have information when it can reasonably be shared; similarly, you deserve to be trusted, unless proven otherwise. Ask for what you need to help make a good decision and/or provide valuable consultation.

STAFF	**Intrapersonal** • Be sure you have a clear idea of which decisions are yours and which rightly belong to others. • Try to listen for and challenge an "us vs. them" mentality, both for yourself and others. • Find common ground around mission and values.
	Interpersonal • Staff may assume at times that shared governance processes exclude staff, and that your voice doesn't matter. The former assumption may be true about some areas, such as promotion and tenure. • The assumption that your voice doesn't matter in shared governance is not true. Find areas to use your voice for the consultation process. While sometimes not top of mind, faculty members often will welcome collaboration with staff around shared interests.
BOT	**Intrapersonal** • Be sure you have a clear idea of which decisions are yours and which rightly belong to others. • Try to listen for and challenge an "us vs. them" mentality, both for yourself and others. • Find common ground around mission and values.
	Interpersonal • The personal/political interest of the board chair/leadership can overextend or minimize the influence of the trustees. • A useful assumption is that unless there are extreme circumstances, shared governance works better if the trustees delegate the operational decisions to other constituencies. • Assume your role is to maintain the financial solvency and mission of the institution, through oversight and supervision of the president and by upholding the institutional bylaws and policies.

STUDENTS	**Intrapersonal** • Be sure you have a clear idea of which decisions are yours and which rightly belong to others. • Try to listen for and challenge an "us vs. them" mentality, both for yourself and others. • Find common ground around mission and values.
	Interpersonal • Your education and learning *is* the mission. Use your voice through shared governance groups and interactions to help others remember to center on the importance of your learning.

"Leader or follower, whichever role you choose to occupy is, quite literally, your job description on the dance floor. What you do with that responsibility will determine who you can dance with." —*Arthur Murray*

Creating Trust

The word *trust* emerges quite often in shared governance conversations at universities. While frequently invoked, the ability to develop and maintain trust is often elusive. At best, trust has a fragile presence, one that can be broken easily. At worst, effective shared governance is sabotaged by the foundational belief that each constituent, especially the administration or the trustees and the faculty and staff, can't trust each other. Because this is more often the case than not, the distrust groups have for each other has often been the motivation to pursue shared governance in the first place. The assumption has been that shared governance is necessary because trust is not possible. Its very purpose can be viewed as the way to safeguard inclusion given the lack of trust.

Shared governance must not be seen as simply a fix for a situation wherein constituents distrust each other. Actual shared governance is impossible without trust, just as a successful dance isn't possible unless both the lead and the follow trust each other and can act in unison.

Yet how can we move beyond the ubiquitous and superficial platitude that "we need to build trust," and actually create trust? How can shared governance work like a Tango, in which each dancer knows their role and trusts the other to act in good faith in the process?

At the end of this chapter, we present a *trust matrix* that summarizes the various forms of trust necessary across constituencies. First, however, trust needs to be deconstructed a bit to be a useful concept.

Let's review five guidelines that will help to frame the creation of trust in shared governance. If each constituent can make a deliberate effort to follow such guidelines, trust becomes possible:

HOW TO CREATE TRUST IN SHARED GOVERNANCE

1. Assume good intentions.
2. Exercise respect for constituents' direct roles.
3. Accept that shared governance is not equally shared and is dependent on the topic or issue being considered.
4. Understand that decision making is tied to budget and AAUP guidelines.
5. Recognize that transformation scares everyone.

1. Assume Good Intentions

First, each constituent must agree to *assume the good intentions* of others. This is hard. It is hard because the default is to assume the opposite. The default is to assume nefarious purposes, which most of the time do not exist. Yet the belief in them is persistent because that belief is often rooted in campus lore. To move forward, we must work to hold each other accountable to this basic guideline of assuming each other's good intentions, especially within our constituency about the members in the other ones.

Here's an example: At one of our campuses, a hiring process was underway for the director of the counseling center. One of the graduate programs regularly placed their students there for a practicum training experience. This was a win-win situation: graduate students received training, under supervision, and they in term provided hours and hours of psychotherapy and testing for the students at the university at no charge. Now a new director needed to be hired; unfortunately, there was little to no communication about that process. The graduate program faculty assumed that the administration didn't care about the needs of their program and students, while the administration assumed that the faculty wanted to control who was hired. Neither was true. Among the faculty members involved, the individual who reminded others that the administration held good intentions was routinely dismissed. Ultimately, after a rather long and difficult process, a suitable hire was made. Had each group assumed good intentions along the way, the process could have involved far fewer emails and meetings, and would not have resulted in leftover hard feelings, which exist to this day.

Trust cannot exist without this foundation of respect. Respect operates on more than one level:

- Individuals earn trust by acting with integrity over time. Actions and words need to be congruent over time. As this occurs repeatedly, others may realize that their decision to *assume good intentions* was the right one to make. Individually, it's crucial that we both give trust and earn trust (by our actions).

- Respect also needs to be attached to the role itself. We need to assume that if the hiring processes have worked, the people in the roles know their jobs. Therefore, we need to respect them in that role.

2. Exercise respect for roles

Trust is a big word and unless deconstructed, it can't exist. Each constituent must first ask: *Trust whom, and about what?*

All constituents need to be clear about each group's role in building the institution's future and *have respect for the wisdom, authority, and responsibility held by each group.* These roles are distinct, and each is crucial:

- Faculty primarily bring expertise about their disciplines, and, therefore, are the authorities on their curriculum and on the qualifications for those who teach in their field. This is validated by the AAUP Redbook. Administrators need to trust faculty to know their disciplines. They need to trust that faculty leadership can understand the data (both quantitative and qualitative) being used to make decisions, and that they can act as thought partners to create better solutions.

- Administrators hold responsibility for the overall health of the university. At their best, administrators are able to see the big picture of how various aspects of the university impact and interact with each other within the broader context of the external operating environment. Faculty need to trust that there is a body of knowledge related to higher education more broadly than their particular discipline, and that many administrators have spent years accumulating and synthesizing that knowledge.

- The Board of Trustees is responsible for the financial solvency of the institution.

- Staff (except on campuses with a faculty senate) and students are often left out of the shared governance equation; however, each group brings wisdom and expertise about the needs of students and can provide insights from their perspectives.

Each of these constituents is needed to create a thriving university. When we are clear on the different roles and commit to treating each other's spheres of responsibility of influence with mutual respect, it becomes easier to assume good intentions and engage in dialogue in good faith.

3. Accept that responsibility and authority are not equally shared

While each constituent group is necessary for effective shared governance, *the responsibility and authority are not equally shared.* Similarly, in the Tango, the dance's lead and follow do not have the same roles or the same authority to decide on the movements of the dance.

'Shared' does not mean that everyone is a decision maker about everything.
This is a bitter truth. Acceptance of this truth is necessary.

Acceptance of this reality can help to build trust; this trust can be developed by a clear definition, understanding, and implementation of *consultation.*

Consultation, at a minimum, is often defined as an activity by which the 'decision maker' gets input from other constituencies. At its best, consultation should include communication among all constituencies, with opportunities to participate in planning and in the resulting activities. Sometimes the lack of equitable responsibility necessitates the sharing of information in ways that do not align with a more formal consultation. For example, we know of one institution that had a $20 million deficit. This information was shared with a handful of faculty leaders, who were asked to hold this in confidence. The faculty were not asked to solve the budget deficit; rather, this contextual information was shared to support consultation about other decisions.

4. Understand that decision making is often tied to budget

Responsibility and authority are most often aligned with budget and other resource stewardship. The constituent that makes the decision is the one that can be fired or removed if the decision results in detrimental effects on the people and the institution, just as the Tango partner who leads is responsible for the overall look and feel of the dance, and for keeping all dancers safe on the dance floor. If poor financial decisions are made, the literal buck stops with the trustees, and often with the administration, as the people charged with implementing the trustees' plans. As much as other groups—tenured faculty, staff, and students in particular—often want to make decisions that have financial implications, their job duties do not include institution-wide budget decisions. While the jobs of staff or untenured faculty may be impacted by poor decisions and budget deficits, they are not held responsible for deficit budgets. Therefore, the decision makers for finances are typically those with budget authority, and with a recognition that finite financial resources imply priorities.

Decisions about curricula rest with those who have subject matter expertise but often intersect with resource allocation. For example, as the content and skills needed in a discipline shift, faculty need to be able to modify their curricula in conjunction with resource reallocation, which is typically the responsibility of administrators. This situation demonstrates the need for administration and faculty to understand their respective roles and responsibilities, because they are making decisions that require mutual trust and consultation.

5. Recognize that transformation scares everyone

Typically, trust is not an issue when operations are status quo. On the other hand, trust becomes very important if a university is trying to innovate and be transformational. Such innovation and transformation are mandatory in the twenty-first century if colleges and universities are to thrive. To build trust, all involved must accept that *transformation is scary to all constituent groups.* Transformation and innovation sound good in theory, but at their core is the potential to create both opportunity and perceived, or actual, danger. For example, even modest changes, such as structural ones, may change job functions, leading to new relationships being built or jobs lost. A realignment of college structures might merge or separate department faculty, create or eliminate a dean position, necessitate moving into new office space, or merge administrative support.

If a transformation is theoretical or doesn't visibly affect us, we are more likely to support it. The closer it impacts us, the scarier it is. Fear—based in a scarcity mentality—creates resistance. And if transformative change is truly innovative, it moves us into uncharted territory, into new previously unseen dance steps, which is scarier. However, if we don't assume that the outcome will be losses, it can also be potentially thrilling—just as learning new dance steps can be exciting and fun.

If we follow the five guidelines above, then we can build the trust without which shared governance cannot operate effectively.

The Dance Steps

What each constituency needs to know about shared governance in relation to building trust

Besides adopting healthier assumptions about shared governance, the second set of steps we need to take in order to learn how to lead and follow well involves building trust.

As you read these, note that you can use these steps in your current role and *also* to help understand the perspectives of others with whom you are working to create effective shared governance.

DANCE STEPS: BUILDING TRUST

ADMINISTRATORS

Intrapersonal

- Remember that you are engaging in shared governance to provide the best possible education for all students.

- Reduce personal defensiveness. Remember that you are engaging in shared governance given your role (e.g., president, VP, director, dean), and that reactions to you are mostly about the role, not about you as a person. Shared governance processes do not work well if you take things too personally and become defensive.

- Subjugate your personal desires and wants to find solutions for the greater good. This includes monitoring the impulse to protect one's turf.

- Develop a comfort with true innovation. Administrators are the ones who typically serve as drivers of innovation and change.

Interpersonal

- Build relationships early and often, when there are no or low stakes. Take or create opportunities to chat about non-work-related topics. This can be accomplished by a five-minute conversation as you pass by an open office door, or the creation of social opportunities for groups.

- Involve those who are affected most by the decisions to be made. If you don't know who is affected, ask.

- Share information about the process and data as soon as possible, and often. This will help to build and maintain credibility. Even if the decision reached is not one that others agree with, they will appreciate knowing how you reached the decision.

- Overshare when the information is not confidential. This will help to build credibility for the times you cannot share information.

- Be aware that building trust starts during the interview process when hired for an administrative role.

- Often, conflicts among administrators are based in a zero-sum mindset, and result in protection of turf regardless of what might work well for students. Make that mindset visible if it's operating, and try to collaborate and create an abundance mindset instead. How will success in one division/unit help other divisions/units?

- Interpersonal processes work better if the chain of command is followed. It can be tempting to try and be the savior and solve the issues. This can quickly undermine shared governance, and implies mistrust and lack of respect for the roles of your subordinates. If someone tries to circumvent and jumps over their supervisor to you, send them back to find a solution with their supervisor before coming to you. Alternatively, be sure to include everyone in the chain of command in any meeting held about the issue.

FACULTY

Intrapersonal

- Remember that you are engaging in shared governance to provide the best possible education for all students. It doesn't work if the focus rests solely on what works for faculty in general, a specific department or program, or an individual faculty member.

- Assess your own influence, whether it is positional or soft power.

- If you are a more senior faculty member, notice how invested you are in keeping the status quo and your comfort level with innovation, technological and otherwise.

- Continue to engage, even when it's hard. Some specific areas to keep in mind that can impact engagement are:

  o Monitor the impulse to withdraw from engagement due to personal agendas or personal slights, such as not feeling heard about a particular decision.

  o Monitor the impulse to approach shared governance with a zero-sum assumption about resources. More for others does not necessarily mean less for you and yours, or that you don't get resources next time.

  o Monitor the impulse to complain off the record, but to not speak up during the process to create changes needed.

Interpersonal

- Build trust with others by staying engaged and involved.

- If you are a faculty in a leadership role, you can facilitate and strongly influence the process and decision.

- Interpersonal processes work better if the chain of command is followed. It can be tempting to jump to higher administration or BOT levels to get the answer you want to solve the issues. This quickly can undermine shared governance and implies mistrust and lack of respect for your

FACULTY	supervisor. Those higher up likely do not have the detailed knowledge of you and your area in order to make an informed decision. Work with your supervisor to find solutions first and involve those higher in the chain of command only when this doesn't resolve the issue. Let your supervisor know you intend to do this. • Consider who your colleagues trust and extend trust based on that, unless proven unfounded or unworthy of your trust. • Listen for the practicality of possible solutions as well as the impact on current practices. • Generate innovative ideas. Even if they don't evolve into practice, thinking creatively will support the entire shared governance process. • Keep in mind the difference between consultation and having the authority to make the decision. If you are not responsible for the area, you probably do not have the authority.
STAFF	**Intrapersonal** • Remember that you are engaging in shared governance to provide the best possible education for all students. This is typically top of mind for staff in student services areas. It doesn't work if the focus rests solely on what works for staff in general, a specific department or program, or an individual staff member. • Assess your own influence, whether it's positional or soft power. • Even if staff members seem to be a 'second thought' in shared governance compared to faculty, use the power and influence you have. **Interpersonal** • Build trust with others by staying engaged and involved. • Work with other staff on shared governance committees/groups to create a united voice and vote. There is power in numbers, and even a minority, with a shared voice, can influence decisions. • Many staff know the intricate details of institutional processes and the needs of students. Bring that knowledge to shared governance interactions.

- Consider who your colleagues trust, and extend trust based on that, unless proven unfounded or unworthy of your trust.

- Listen for the practicality of possible solutions as well as the impact on current practices.

- Generate innovative ideas. Even if they don't evolve into practice, thinking creatively will support the entire shared governance process.

Intrapersonal

- Remember that you are engaging in shared governance to provide the best possible education for all students.

- Embrace innovation as you consider the health and future of the university.

Interpersonal

- Trust the administrator you hired (the president) and those they hired to run the daily operations.

- Recognize the power dynamics embedded in the relationship between you and the president. Set clear expectations for that role, including which decisions are delegated to them, and which ones you expect to make .

- Encourage the president to tell you both good and bad news, without spin.

- Rise above the 'us vs. them' mentality that often exists between administrators and faculty. Conflicts between the BOT and faculty can slow down or derail effective shared governance.

- Respect the knowledge faculty and staff members hold about their and their students' needs.

- Relationships with faculty and staff can be friendly, and by design, are limited. They are very aware of the power embedded in the trustee role, and information provided to you is almost always filtered by that awareness.

BOT

STUDENTS	**Intrapersonal** • Educate yourself about shared governance, so that you know the processes, and the roles and responsibilities of each constituency. • Think about the needs of all students, not just your own. Talk to students who are outside your inner circle to find out what they need. **Interpersonal** • You will be part of committees and groups that discuss confidential information. Maintain that confidentiality—do not tell anyone, even one other person. • You will need to earn the trust of the other constituents. Many administrators/faculty/staff do not think you can be trusted to keep confidentiality. • At the same time, they should recognize and know the importance of your involvement and perspective to make good decisions, so speak up. • You will earn more credibility if you can include the needs of many students, not just your own experience and needs.

The Trust Matrix

Trust is complex in shared governance processes. It can depend on the situational context and the power dynamics between constituent groups, given the authority that varies across each group.

In the *trust matrix* shown on pages 28-29, you will find tips to help each pair of constituencies think about what you can understand about each other, as well as tips for what each group can trust about other members in your group. For example:

- In the first row, the *italicized* text provides some guidance for students about what they can trust about administrators.

- In the first row, the **bold** text below is a suggestion for what administrators might trust about each other.

In each cell in this matrix, the word *trust* implies the willingness and need to understand one reality and/or perspective.

	ADMINISTRATORS	FACULTY	STAFF	BOT	STUDENTS
ADMINISTRATORS	Trust that each division's leaders have expertise and a unique view of the university.	Trust that administrators see a broader view than most faculty see. This view may help to see the unintended consequences of any decision.	Trust that administrators see a broader view than most staff see. This view may help to see the unintended consequences of any decision. Many administrators see and value the role of staff.	Trust administrators to run the daily operations of the university.	*Trust that administrators want the best education for students.*
FACULTY	Trust that faculty leadership will hold confidentiality. Trust that faculty leadership can understand data and use it well for decision making.	Trust that relationships built among colleagues will serve to make shared governance more effective.	Trust that faculty appreciate the work done with students by staff.	Trust that faculty have both a healthy respect and fear of the BOT. Trust that faculty want to have 'face time' with the BOT.	Trust that faculty really know their discipline and are excited to share that with students.
STAFF	Trust that staff leadership will hold confidentiality. Trust that staff leadership can understand data and use it well for decision making.	Trust that staff spend quality time with students and bring that important perspective to shared governance.	Trust that other staff also feel invisible by the shared governance structures and processes.	Trust that the staff have a healthy respect and fear of the BOT.	Trust that the staff, especially student support staff, really are focused on student well-being and see students holistically.

	ADMINISTRATORS	FACULTY	STAFF	BOT	STUDENTS
BOT	Trust that the BOT will make good decisions if provided the data needed.	Trust that the BOT respects faculty, based on their own experiences as a college student.	Trust that staff are mostly invisible to BOT.	Trust that all BOT members are committed to the welfare of the university.	Trust that the BOT really wants to hear directly from students about their experiences.
STUDENTS	Trust that students can hold confidences if asked to. Trust students to know what they need.	Trust that students bring a perspective to shared governance that is sometimes missed by others.	Trust that students will often bring up issues to staff that they are reluctant to share with others on campus.	Trust that the students do not understand the role of the BOT. Yet trust that current students can provide a valuable perspective as a BOT member.	Trust that other students may share some perspectives, and many will not. Talk to others who are not similar to learn more, to inform student leaders work in shared governance.

As mentioned in the preface, each chapter will close with Self-Reflection questions. You may use these to explore the content from the chapter privately, or you can use the answers for group discussions. The group discussions may be conducted with members of your constituency group, across constituencies, or both.

SELF-REFLECTION

To explore this chapter's ideas further, consider the following questions related to the roles and assumptions about the shared governance process.

1. What will help you to stay focused on the ultimate goal of quality education for all students?

2. Notice what triggers your defensiveness. Once you notice any patterns, explore what fears are operating, and what feels threatening to you. Take a step back and assess the likelihood of the danger. Is the danger actual or merely perceived? You can use this space to reflect on a time when your defensiveness was triggered:

3. Think about times you have experienced change. What was your initial response? How did the change ultimately affect you? If it was exciting, did it live up to your expectations? If it was scary, did the worst case actually happen? Did you survive or thrive or something in between?

4. Reflect on your comfort level with the status quo vs. innovation:

5. Do an honest assessment of the status of your current relationships at work. How might you tend to these relationships and mend any breaches, starting with low-stakes collaborations?

6. Consider the flawed assumptions discussed on pages 12-13. Which of these assumptions resonated with you as you read the chapter? How might you notice when they are operating for you? Once you notice them, how can you challenge yourself to consider alternatives and substitute flawed assumptions with more adaptive ones?

7. Review the more adaptive guidelines about shared governance discussed on pages 19-22. Think about which ones are easier or harder for you to embrace.

8. Review the *trust matrix* on the preceding pages. Next time you think about trust or mistrust, deconstruct the idea: Ask yourself, "Trust about what, specifically?" and, using the matrix, notice where trust exists already. You can use the following space to jot down your thoughts:

CHAPTER TWO:
FILLING YOUR DANCE CARD—
YOUR SPHERE OF INFLUENCE AND POWER
DYNAMICS

"Pretend that every single person you meet has a sign around his or her neck that says, 'Make me feel important.' Not only will you succeed in sales, you will succeed in life." —Mary Kay Ash

---

TOPICS COVERED IN THIS CHAPTER:

- Power dynamics and the ability to influence others

- Impact of intersecting identities on shared governance

Engaging Others

The success of a dance partnership is dependent on the dancers' ability to support and enhance each other. This means that partners are willing to put in the necessary time and effort to learn their dance steps, practice repeatedly, work through challenging moves, and be supportive and patient if the other partner struggles or stumbles. In the event that the dance team must dissolve (for example, if one partner is injured or retires from professional dancing), the remaining partner will have more influence to persuade a new dance partner if they have a reputation for being professional, hardworking, cooperative, and supportive.

The ideas offered in this chapter will be relevant when either:

- You are influencing others, and you are *not* the decision maker.

- You *are* the decision maker, and you want to build a modified consensus through consultation, prior to making a decision.

Sometimes the power dynamics in relationships relevant to shared governance are structural, related to your role. Sometimes, you might have 'soft power'—the ability to influence others—based on your personal and/or professional relationship with them. In both cases, you have the ability to influence others. How large or small that influence extends will depend on many factors, including how many relationships you have built through working together on high- and low-stakes initiatives, your longevity at the institution, your embodiment, and your own approach to power. We will first discuss the authority and power prescribed by your role, and then look at how your embodiment and intersecting identities impact the power dynamics in your shared governance interactions.

Positional and Structural Power Dynamics

Shared governance is all about power dynamics. It specifies the rules and structures to make the power dynamics transparent. To be effective, shared governance power dynamics must be about the empowerment of all involved, not about control over others. What makes these power dynamics so complex is that within the context of collaboration and empowerment, someone (whether an individual or a group) is authorized to be the decision maker.

The crux of the power dynamic of shared governance is how to empower and collaborate (i.e., listen and consult) *and* make decisions. Sometimes, the decisions are difficult ones to make. Ultimately, the final decisions—and therefore, the control—rest at the board, system, or state level. Even if an individual such as the university president makes the decision, they are acting in their role on behalf of the institution, not as an individual. The same is true when the faculty are making decisions about curriculum or personnel matters. They are acting on behalf of the institution. All decision makers within shared governance need to keep that in mind, trying as much as possible to put individual, personal desires aside to make decisions to serve the greater good.

Ultimately, effective shared governance is a formal mechanism that can serve to promote equity and inclusion. It can lead to policies and practices that are truly inclusive—that is, the voices of those who are impacted are equally valued and heard in the process. Hopefully, decisions made will take into account the need for equity, with an acknowledgement that shared governance decisions will likely impact each constituency differently. If shared governance processes can embrace an equity-minded approach, they can be used to innovate higher education practices.

Getting clarity on your role and others' roles for each decision

As you think about engaging others, first you must have clarity about your role, then clarity about the roles of others. Be clear on where you, in your role, have decision-making power. Each stakeholder in shared governance has a different role, and each role has responsibilities for certain decisions. Each stakeholder has the need to engage in consultation. As discussed before, decisions often are made by those who are accountable for the results, whose job duties and success depend on the outcomes. And some roles, such as administrators and trustees, need to seek out consultation, while other roles—those of faculty, staff, and students—need to engage authentically in consultation. In the areas of curriculum and promotion/tenure, faculty need to consult each other in order to make their recommendations to administrators. Be clear about your role in the decision-making process and in the need for consultation.

Also, be clear about others' roles. This clarity is important in general as well as for any given policy or practice under consideration. Clarity will help to locate and ground you as you engage and influence others.

Building relationships

Building relationships prior to high-stakes areas for shared governance is fundamental. Many of you will have the opportunity to build those relationships through informal social interactions or low-stakes decisions. If you are able, seek out ways to connect with others by taking 'the long walk home from lunch.' Although this is not always possible given remote work in our post-COVID-19 environment, when you and your colleagues are present in person, take a 15-minute break to stick your head in someone's door to say hello and ask about them and about their life. Ask someone to grab a coffee. Really listen to them about non-work-related matters, and remember what they tell you. Or, just a bit more formally, when working on low-stakes committee work, be gracious and flexible. Support others to make decisions to show that you respect and value them, their experience, and their ideas. Once you have a relationship, it will be easier to have more difficult conversations when consulting about higher-stakes shared governance policies and practices.

Your longevity at the institution will impact who you have influence with, and how you have influence. If you have the luxury of having been at an institution for many years, you probably already have some foundational social relationships, especially if you started as, or still are, peers. If you are newer to an institution, it is even more important that you create some informal opportunities to connect, soon and often. Sometimes longevity can make shared-governance relationships more difficult, as early conflicts can haunt your entire career at an institution.

Shared Governance and Intersecting Identities

The shared governance Tango exists in a larger societal context of intersecting and embodied identities.

As with all interactions, we must consider both the structural power given to specific roles and the intersectional identities of who might be involved. Black, Indigenous, and People of Color (BIPOC) in all roles need to navigate assumptions about race/ethnicity in the shared governance process, just as women, transgender, and nonbinary people need to navigate assumptions about gender.

Take a moment to consider this example. A top candidate for Athletic Director is a former NBA star, and the search committee places him at the top of their list for hiring. The president, through informal and confidential reference calls, finds out that this candidate has been fired at previous jobs for sexual misconduct. The president declines to offer him the job, instead offering it to the second candidate, a woman. Consider:

- How might this be perceived by the search committee and the campus if the president is White and male?

- What if the president is a White woman?

- A Black woman?

- How might each scenario be perceived if the successful candidate is a woman of Color? A White woman?

How would the embodiment of each of these fictitious presidents impact how they navigate the shared governance implications of their decision? As president, each has structural power and authority. However, their embodiment likely impacts how their decision might be interpreted by the search committee and the larger campus community. These interpretations might then extend to assumptions about the president's respect for the shared governance process for this job hire, and more broadly.

Influence and intersecting identities

Your ability to influence others in shared governance is impacted by your identities, both visible and invisible. Your embodiment—the often-visible identities, such as race/ethnicity, gender, some disabilities, and age—will impact how you are able to build relationships. For any given shared governance policy and practice, your voice will be heard differently by those who share your identity from how it is heard by those who do not.

Imagine that you are on a task force to revise Title IX policies. If you identify as and appear to be a woman, how will your insights about sexual assault be heard differently than the insights by a male? Now imagine a senate meeting in which the members are asked to adopt a statement about hate crimes on campus. Will BIPOC and White members' voices be heard similarly? In general, be aware that if you are speaking up with a visible identity about issues that relate to that identity, your colleagues may give more weight to your perspectives, increasing your ability to influence. However, the reverse can also be true. Your ideas may be seen as self-serving.

Your influence is also affected by your non-visible identities, which may or may not be known by your colleagues. These include but are not limited to class status, sexual orientation, gender identity, some disabilities or chronic illnesses, and religion. These less-visible identities may be known or suspected, or you may decide to disclose them when you believe it's important.

Imagine if the policy or practice under discussion relates to contracting for textbook sales. Imagine that most of the people in the room are upper-middle class and came from family backgrounds at that same level. However, you grew up in a family that lived paycheck to paycheck. What would you feel comfortable disclosing, to help your colleagues to understand the financial pressures experienced by many students? What do you gain (or lose) by disclosing this to influence this discussion and decision?

Clarifying your own approach to power

Lastly, to use your sphere of influence with intentionality, you need to examine your approach to power/control. Here are some questions to consider:

- Do you believe you have the power to influence others?

- Does your power rest with your formal role, or with your relationships with others, or both?

- How comfortable are you with your power to influence?

- When are you likely to use that power, or not?

- Do you subscribe to a top-down model of control, regardless of where you are in the hierarchy? How does that fit, or not, with the approach at your institution?

(We have provided some space in the Self-Reflection on pages 41-44 to journal your responses to these questions.)

Shared governance lives within a hierarchy; depending on your role, your ability to influence others will be impacted by where you are in that hierarchy. Even when considering the use of soft power, some people will see you in your role rather than seeing you as a person. You will need to examine your own beliefs about this, as well. Consider a couple of different situations:

- First, when you are having a conversation with your supervisor, how do you word your ideas? How tentatively or forcefully do you state your ideas?

- Imagine discussing those same ideas with a peer or with someone who reports to you. How might your approach vary? If it varies, you are attending to the hierarchy and the power dynamics embedded within it.

Each of us needs to embrace our ability to influence and find ways to use that ability without trying to control others. Embracing it means that we continue to engage even when it's hard to see results, hard to feel empowered ourselves, hard to feel heard, or hard to not impose our will on others. Shared governance only works when we each use our knowledge and bring both our own listening and our persuasive skills as part of the process.

FOR MORE ON DEVELOPING AN EQUITY-MINDED LENS

Can our environment, our institutions, be a landscape in which every living being thrives? Can we create the best possible soil to nourish all, to allow the potential within each of us to flourish? We believe the answer is yes.

To explore how to develop an equity-minded lens, and the very complex dynamics around interesting identities, please see our book *Courageous Gardening*:

https://www.academicimpressions.com/product/equity-minded-leadership-higher-education/

The Dance Steps

What each constituency needs to know about shared governance in relation to spheres of influence

Keeping in mind 1) the need to be equity-minded and 2) the balance of empowerment for all with 3) the very real need for decisions to be made, let's delve a bit more into how to be an effective lead and an effective follow in the shared governance Tango. We offer the following guidelines for each constituency about their sphere of influence. You will note that some of these steps are unique to a specific constituency, while others apply to all. Remember, you can use these steps in your current role and *also* to help you to understand the perspectives of others with whom you are working to create effective shared governance.

While influencing others, the bottom line is to focus on the impact of the practice and/or policy on students. Bring this perspective into the conversation and remind yourself and others if the focus drifts. This perspective can help to 'center' decisions, redirecting our attention back to the academic mission.

DANCE STEPS: INFLUENCING OTHERS

Intrapersonal

- Many administrators have doctorates and expertise in an academic area, maybe as former faculty members. Monitor yourself that you don't slip into that role during shared governance processes. For example, some administrators have been known to want to make decisions about curriculum in their field, when this should be left to faculty to design.

- Check your entitlement and embrace humility. If you are in a role with a lot of power for decision making, it can be difficult to consider that you may not have the 'right' answer.

Interpersonal

- Administrators can strongly influence shared governance by carefully crafting the committee or task force charge. Writing a good charge to the committee or task force is an art. It needs to include a timeline, expectations about data use, and guidance about the deliverables. Please see the Appendix for a template.

- Hand in hand with the charge, a carefully selected membership is important, if possible. While it can be tempting to select those you believe might align with your views, a stronger membership will

ADMINISTRATORS

include those who think critically. A diversity of views by people working on a project will result in a more effective result and is in the spirit of shared governance. For elaboration on these ideas, consider reading our book *Running the Race*: https://www.academicimpressions.com/product/running-the-race/.

FACULTY

Intrapersonal

- While there is a 'top-down' hierarchy regarding organizational charts, these do not apply to shared governance. Think of your role as one of concentric circles or varying spheres of influence. Engage purposefully with the areas that fall under faculty to make the primary decision; note areas in which faculty hold a primary role for consultation; and spend less time and focus on the ones that allow for input but are not central to the role of faculty.

- Engagement is easier if we remember that each faculty member can make a difference and a contribution to shared governance. Manage frustration, low morale, and exhaustion, since these make it more difficult to engage.

- Faculty often have far more longevity at an institution than administrators. This longevity carries a knowledge of history and a passion:

  o Try to use history judiciously, but not to get stuck in the 'old days' or 'how it used to be'.

  o Passion is compelling when influencing others. Embrace your passion for the institution and its students.

Interpersonal

- Use your influence to gently correct other faculty who may need more information, are speaking from a non-inclusive viewpoint, or may be making statements that are not accurate.

- Faculty work with students across many groups and identities. As you think about 'students' in shared governance, remind others that there is no one 'student.' Rather, use your experience to remind others to consider which students are included, and which are not during shared governance conversations.

STAFF	**Intrapersonal** • Overcome your fear of speaking up. You may be tempted to stay silent and be less involved, due to fear of job loss. Try to focus on the important contribution you can make to shared governance. Your voice is needed, as staff often have more contact with students and in more contexts than in other constituencies. **Interpersonal** • Other constituencies will rely on you for information about the specific student populations with which you work.
BOT	**Intrapersonal** • Monitor how you use the power of your role as trustee. Try not to overstep the purview of your role in shared governance. • Check your entitlement and embrace humility. Being a trustee is the role with ultimate power for decision making. Always consider that you may not have the 'right' answer, as you rarely will know all the details needed. **Interpersonal** • The scope of influence (and actual decision-making power) varies from the statutory power given the BOT. • The personal/political interest of the board chair/leadership can overextend or minimize the influence of the trustees. • In general, the work of the BOT should be more symbolic than operational. That is, do not micromanage. Operational focus is disrespectful of the expertise and roles of the faculty, staff, and administration. Let them do their jobs. • In any shared governance interactions, even seemingly informal conversations, others will always see you as a trustee. Power dynamics will impact how you are heard, so pick your words carefully. Do not imply decisions outside of the shared governance process.

STUDENTS	Intrapersonal • Be confident. It can be intimidating to be in a room with faculty, staff, and administrators. Remember that you are an equal member on a committee, with the same voting rights of others.
	Interpersonal • Your voice will help the other committee members to focus on meeting student needs, which should be the central criteria for decisions.

SELF-REFLECTION

To explore this chapter's ideas further, consider the following questions related to the relationships in the shared governance process.

1. Identify your current sphere of influence. Whose 'ear' do you have?

2. Given your current role, make a list of areas in which you have decision making authority and responsibility:

3. Identify other people with whom you want or need to develop a relationship. Make a plan to intentionally and informally get to know them:

4. As mentioned in the chapter, take some time to think about your relationship to power dynamics. Do you believe you have the power to influence others? Does your power rest with your formal role, or your relationships with others, or both? (That is, in what ways do you hold either/both *positional power* or *relational/soft power*?)

5. How comfortable are you with your power to influence? When are you likely to use it, or not?

6. Do you subscribe to a top-down model of control, regardless of where you are in the hierarchy? How does that fit, or not, with the approach at your institution?

7. Consider how you engage with your supervisor compared to peers. Use these observations to gain insight about hierarchical power dynamics:

8. Sometimes, loss of privilege and entitlement leads to defensiveness. If this is the case, do an honest self-assessment of your own sense of entitlement. If being equity-minded is important to you, examine ways to notice when entitlement is operating for you, and take steps to decrease it:

9. Consider your longevity at the institution and how this impacts your sphere of influence. Consider how it impacts your approach to history and future initiatives:

CHAPTER THREE:
STRUCTURAL ISSUES—
THE BALLROOM AND MUSIC

"Think outside the box, collapse the box, and take a f**king sharp knife to it." —*Banksy*

> TOPICS COVERED IN THIS CHAPTER:
>
> • Impact of structures on shared governance
>
> • Defining and using consultation in shared governance

Overview

Every Argentine Tango dance includes the same elements: the *embrace, walking, figures,* and *codes of conduct.* These four elements provide a structure from which there are infinite possibilities to create and express an artistic dance. The dance itself typically takes place in a ballroom, to a specific type of music.

Similarly, in shared governance, the committees or the senates for various constituencies are the places where it occurs. Ask anyone about shared governance at a university and, invariably, they will mention committees and the necessary representation of all constituents. Unlike the Tango, however, institutional shared governance's insistence on committees and/or senates, as well as representational membership, can have the inverse effect, *limiting* the possibilities for input or effective solutions.

Additionally, policies are like the sheet music and musical notes played by the musicians. They form the backdrop by which people interact.

Bodies that are considered shared governance are typically voted on by the constituency of the whole. That is, a faculty, staff, or student senate is voted on by all the members of the faculty, students, or staff, and in theory, anyone can serve. Some institutional committees are also voted on by the entire constituency, such a budget committee to which the faculty, staff, and student groups each elect representatives to serve. A non-shared governance committee might be appointed for either ongoing work or for a specific task (the latter is sometimes called a task force).

To be clear, we believe that representation is necessary. We believe that the constituencies most impacted by decisions need to have a strong voice in deliberations. We also consider that administration needs a voice, and we acknowledge that administrators are often the decision makers. We also believe that to be innovative—to reach effective solutions for all—institutions should consider creating work groups/committees related to areas of responsibility, rather than rely on formulas for representation. For example, to assume one needs a certain number of people representing each constituency may ignore the need for representation based on expertise or who will be most affected by the decisions. Sometimes, the formal shared governance senate or committee may be the best deliberative body; other times, it may not be. Institutions need the flexibility built into their shared governance protocols to form new structures to meet emerging needs.

Working creatively within existing structures

When working within given structures, institutions can develop norms that invite creativity. For example:

- An institution might ask committees to consider any proposal in parallel, rather than sequentially, so that the timeline is compressed.

- Some institutions have expanded the definition of shared governance groups to allow for the creation of committees/task forces rather than always using the elected traditional structures—and have specified under which conditions this will occur.

- We can also be more creative with timing. For example, rather than assuming that nothing can be done over the summer, we can conduct deliberations during that time, perhaps virtually, with compensation for those who serve who are on a nine-month contract.

Senates

Senates are the most utilized shared governance structure. They often represent a constituency, such as faculty, staff, or students. When these constituencies are represented by separate senates, each voice can be used to bring unique perspectives. When the various senates communicate among themselves to speak with one voice, these messages and perspectives can be used to harmoniously blend and empower all constituencies represented.

We have each worked on campuses in which each senate is separate, and on campuses in which the faculty and staff senates are combined. In both cases, the power dynamics resulted in faculty voices carrying more weight. During discussions of joint senates, faculty spoke more often and for longer than staff. Staff members often deferred to the faculty, although at times there were well-respected staff to whom faculty listened. Attention to these power dynamics is important in shared governance, as staff often advocate more effectively for students' needs. We encourage institutions to create processes which lift up staff voices to be on par with those of faculty.

Student senates seem to vary in power. At one student-centered institution where we worked, the student senate representatives were important members of most shared governance committees. Students were very involved in issues that impacted them, and if they were not in agreement, the initiative was often delayed or stopped. On another campus where we worked, the opposite occurred. Student representatives were in attendance in name only.

If the issues being deliberated involve students' learning, inside and outside the classroom, we believe that student voices should be actively sought and empowered. When students understand the full picture, we have found that they make good decisions, and that they are able to communicate their reasoning and the decisions that have been made to their constituency effectively.

Factors that impact structures and power dynamics

The structural components of shared governance vary in the number and size of membership across institutions. Larger institutions may see more complexity in these structures. That is, a larger institution may have multiple committees and more representative members on each committee, while smaller campuses may have proportionally smaller numbers involved in shared governance. Since communication is such an important part of shared governance, one must take complexity into account when crafting a communication plan about the input sought and the decisions reached via a shared governance process. Typically, communication plans need to be managed by administrators, with input from the various constituencies about their participation and about the areas of responsibility they will assume. (See Chapter Five for more on communication in shared governance.)

Shared governance structures also vary based on voting rights. We have each served on campuses in which administrators were expected to attend senate meetings—sometimes with voting rights, and other times, without. Attending without voting rights is referred to as *ex-officio*. By contrast, we have also worked at institutions that forbade administrators from attending senate meetings unless expressly invited.

Consider for a moment the power dynamics at play in the different situations described above. If we view shared governance as a Tango, what does it mean to dance alone? What does it mean for one partner to make all the decisions about the choreography? Or to be invited to dance without being able to participate in most of the rehearsals?

If administrators can vote, the groups must monitor the impact that the visibility of those votes can have on others—administrators often hold power over resources. Written votes may help to minimize the power dynamics of a visible vote or a visible preference by administrators. If, however, administrators are not invited in until the final discussions, then valuable information provided by them may not have been available to inform the voting members' decisions.

Consultation

Most shared governance structures are composed of elected membership. At times, however, working groups may be composed of a mix of appointed members and/or those elected/chosen by standing committees/senates. Consultation, an important step in all shared governance, will be more complex as one moves from elected, recognized bodies to those that are appointed or formed to address a specific issue. What counts as consultation? Informal conversations in hallways? Discussions and communications with non-elected groups? Sometimes, if members are appointed, constituents do not believe consultation has occurred unless formal bodies are also included.

We encourage consultation to include both formal and informal structures.

At several institutions, we noticed that communicating with formal structures, such as senates, often provided the members with information, but that information never reached the broader constituencies. When decisions were then announced campus-wide, most people were surprised at the outcomes. Administrators had thought that the elected representatives were telling their member constituencies, but these constituencies had not been informed or involved by their elected representatives. (See Chapter Five for more ideas about communication.)

The faculty union

If campuses have faculty unions, these can act as informal structures that impact shared governance. Faculty senates can act as independent voices or can be conflated with unions. Both cases complicate shared governance, as knowing which body should be consulted and/or make decisions for its members can be confusing. Unions are not part of shared governance structures on most campuses. Their input has a role, but union consultation will be more effectively used as a parallel process to shared governance deliberations.

The accrediting body

Lastly, one important group in shared governance is the accrediting body. They are the producer for the dance itself, responsible for how all aspects of the performance come together. Some initiatives that move through shared governance at the institutional level, such as new geographic locations, new types of degrees, or changes in mission, need to involve accreditors. Each accrediting organization has staff who are assigned to an institution to provide technical assistance. Involving them early on for major institutional changes is important. After all of the work within shared governance on a campus, you will want to be sure that any new directions are agreeable to the accrediting body—just as the dancers in a Tango need to make sure the musical producer is on board with any new dance steps.

As we end this chapter, it's important to mention policies. Remember that policies are created by institutions and can be modified if needed to become more useful and equitable. If well done, they can help provide guidance to engage in effective shared governance processes—like a beautifully choreographed dance. Poorly done or confusing policies can create chaotic interactions and movements, resulting in stepped-on toes or kicked shins.

ASSUMPTIONS TO CHALLENGE

Structures seem to be a primary focus when thinking about shared governance. They are built on the status quo assumptions of constituencies having separate but conflictual interests. Given these roots in history and hegemony, how can we create innovation within the shared governance process?

The Dance Steps

What each constituency needs to know about shared governance in relation to structures

We offer the following guidelines for each constituency about possible assumptions that can help or harm the shared governance process. Remember, you can use these steps in your current role and *also* to help understand the perspectives of others with whom you are working to create effective shared governance.

As you identify assumptions during your shared governance processes—both your own assumptions and others'—making these explicit can help to examine them. If these assumptions are operating, they are important to note so that they can be questioned if they are inaccurate or embedded into the process if they are accurate.

DANCE STEPS: STRUCTURAL ISSUES

| | **Intrapersonal**
• Monitor your input and visible preferences when serving on shared governance committees/senates. Listen more and speak less. Provide clarifying and accurate data and information when needed.

Interpersonal
• Include representatives, as much as possible, at your regular meetings within your unit. Trust that they can keep items confidential if needed.
• Use working groups to do preliminary work ahead of time of elected shared governances committees. This work can then be shared with the elected groups to help their deliberations go more quickly and be data-informed.
• Consider the use of external consultants to help shepherd big or potentially contentious projects.
• Be familiar with handbooks and policies, and use them to inform the process.
• Develop communication plans based on the size and complexity of the shared governance structures. Assume that you will need to use both the formal communication via the structures, as well as informal messaging across the different modalities. Involve the elected shared governance bodies to provide input into and participate in this plan. |
| **ADMINISTRATORS** | **Intrapersonal**
• Monitor which faculty speak at shared governance meetings and those who keep quiet. Help empower all faculty to have a voice. |

FACULTY	• How do you define 'faculty?' Does your definition include only tenure track? Do you include lecturers and adjuncts when you think of 'faculty?' How can you keep a broader definition in mind when participating in shared governance discussions?
	Interpersonal
	• Monitor which faculty are elected to shared governance bodies. Encourage election processes to be inclusive and representative of all faculty.
	• If electing others to serve, consider how to elect/nominate faculty who have interest or knowledge, rather than the 'known' faculty leadership.
	• Department chairs hold important positions to help advocate for their faculty. Consider the best use of their (limited) time in the shared governance structures. When are they the best representative of the department, and when might it be better to involve others?
	• Whether unionized or not, there are often norms about contractual obligations of faculty during summer. Consider which issues are important to work on during summer, and the impact of delay, if any.
STAFF	**Intrapersonal**
	• In shared governance meetings that include all constituencies, notice your comfort level with speaking. Do you speak up regardless or do you defer to certain groups (such as faculty or administrators)?
	Interpersonal
	• Monitor which staff are elected to shared governance bodies. Encourage election processes to be inclusive and representative of all staff.
	• If there is no formal role for staff in a shared governance structure, work with faculty leaders or equity-minded administrators to either/both modify the structures to include staff or develop processes in which staff voices are included more directly.
BOT	**Intrapersonal**
	• Have clarity about the strategic role of a trustee—and leave the operational tasks to the administration, faculty, and staff.

BOT	**Interpersonal** • Limit your direct communication with faculty and staff. Use administrators to manage the strategic directions set by the BOT. • There are both benefits and challenges to include faculty members as trustees, or to attend meetings as non-voting delegates. What is the current composition for your institution's BOT?[2] • Include faculty senate representation during open sessions at each BOT meeting. Use this time to discuss strategic directions that all can agree to and participate in their success.
STUDENTS	**Intrapersonal** • Analyze your comfort with speaking in shared governance meetings. Power dynamics with faculty in the room can be difficult to manage. Speak up! All decisions need to ultimately serve you and your education. **Interpersonal** • Monitor which students are elected to shared governance bodies. Encourage election processes to be inclusive and representative of all students (e.g., ethnicity, age, generation in college, veteran status). • When serving on a committee, read the agenda and materials ahead of time. Take that information to other students and get their input. Your vote should reflect all students, not just your own opinion or needs.

---

[2] See https://agb.org/knowledge-center/board-fundamentals/board-roles-and-responsibilities/ from AGB for more information.

CHAPTER FOUR:
OUTCOMES—STRATEGIC VS. OPERATIONS FOCUSED

"I dwell in Possibility." —Emily Dickinson

> TOPICS COVERED IN THIS CHAPTER:
>
> - Shared governance and operational effectiveness
>
> - The role of shared governance in setting strategic directions
>
> - Using shared governance to manage opposing views of institutional priorities

Overview

People dance the Tango for a variety of reasons. Some do it for the pure pleasure of the Tango, while others engage in serious and lucrative competitions. Rehearsals can include the painstaking effort to break down the dance into each step and then practicing each small part, before putting them together to create a beautiful and expressive whole. Practicing each step can be tedious, if one can't yet see how each step fits into the whole, final dance. Someone—whether a dancer, a choreographer, or the musical arranger—must be able to see the finished product while working on each separate part.

The components of a shared governance process are similar. Sometimes the task at hand is to use the shared governance process to focus on a specific policy or practice. Often, it is not clear how that one policy or practice in isolation plays an important part in the overall mission or vision of the institution. This *operations* focus in shared governance is crucial to the effectiveness of the institution in carrying out its mission. Other times, the mission itself or the institution's overall objectives are themselves the *strategic* focus of a shared governance process, and that process is used to create meaningful paradigm shifts in the mission or in the institution's vision or values.

Operations-focused shared governance

Operations-focused shared governance is more concrete. Standing committees with prescribed membership and defined processes typically are charged with much of the operational shared governance. On most campuses, committees of this type might include a budget committee, a policy committee, curriculum committees, rank and tenure committees, a grievance committee, a calendar committee, a parking committee, and more. Most of shared governance dwells in the land of the operational.

Strategic shared governance

As the name suggests, an institution's strategic planning process can fall under strategic shared governance. That process will likely use both standing committees and specially-formed work groups. While we note the possibility that this process can create a paradigm shift, there is no guarantee that a strategic planning process will result in anything other than a continuation, or rewording, of the past goals, norms, values, and mission. We have found in our work across many institutions that there is strong pressure to preserve the hegemonic norm. Shared governance is often used to create the *appearance* of stakeholders' involvement and input in strategic plans, and then no substantive change occurs.

Strategic work may also emerge during a crisis—when the routine no longer works. In fact, crises may create urgency, motivation, and opportunities for strategic change that has needed to occur but otherwise would not occur. In a crisis, each constituency may have more motivation to use shared governance processes as intended: to bring together the various constituent perspectives to solve problems that affect the overall health of the institution. The COVID-19 pandemic is a good example of this, when a disruption of 'business as usual' necessitated a paradigm shift in the modalities for the delivery of education. As we write this book in 2024, the COVID-19 pandemic not only has continued to disrupt the status-quo delivery of education but has also created financial effects that have exacerbated a rapid financial divide between fiscally strong institutions and those that will close, merge, or downsize significantly in the next few years. Truly strategic thinking might have helped failing institutions to survive; the lack of strategic innovation indicates how difficult it is for shared governance to be nimble and strategic on most campuses.

If shared governance operates in strategic discussions, a focus on the institutional mission can help to keep the discussion productive. Also, a knowledge of and commitment to regulatory guidelines (such as accreditation) and ethical behavior can assist those involved to work together collaboratively and effectively. Disagreement and resistance is expected and necessary as the discussion moves toward new ways of being and thinking strategically. Keep in mind that if everyone is in agreement, it is unlikely that the ideas are strategically challenging the current norms and operations. Think of that discomfort as a sign that the process is leading to potentially new and innovative ideas. Even if not acted on, this type of exploration can result in creative solutions.

Lastly, the outcomes that result from strategic shared governance can result in progressive solutions—some of which may be innovative and others not. Operations-focused shared governance may form the majority of shared governance processes; however, using shared governance to create strategic changes is a difficult and necessary opportunity in the current higher education landscape.

The Dance Steps

What each constituency needs to know about being strategic and intentional

We offer the following guidelines for each constituency about possible assumptions or actions that can help or harm the shared governance process. Remember, you can use these steps in your current role and *also* to help understand the perspectives of others with whom you are working to create effective shared governance.

As you identify assumptions during your shared governance processes—both your own assumptions and others'—making these explicit can help to examine them. If these assumptions are operating, they are important to note so that they can be questioned if they are inaccurate, or embedded into the process if they are accurate.

DANCE STEPS: OUTCOMES—STRATEGIC VS. OPERATIONAL

ADMINISTRATORS	**Intrapersonal**
	
	• We have noticed that many administrators default to a structural solution to solve problems that might really be a performance issue. If you have used structural solutions (e.g., modifying the organizational chart, etc.), reflect on which problems these solutions solved, if any.
	
	Interpersonal
	
	• Innovation needs champions and cheerleaders. Find and cultivate them for each strategic process.
	
	• Typically, it is the administrator's job to set the deliverables and timeline.
	    ○ Consider how a reasonable length of time varies between operational and strategic processes.
	    ○ An operational deliverable is typically easier to measure. Consider how to measure when a strategic goal has been reached.
	
	• Encourage others to think in more strategic ways by helping the discussion to focus on student needs, rather than on numbers. Remind yourself and others why you are here.
	
	• Invite radical ideas from others.
	
	• Frame new strategic directions as pilots. Help others to let go of perfectionism in strategic solutions.
	
	• Engage in modified consensus to reach decisions. *Modified consensus* means that everyone is heard but recognizes that often decisions do not have 100% agreement.

FACULTY	**Intrapersonal** • If tenured, you can take more risks. Use this to support innovation. **Interpersonal** • Ask for a clearly framed charge from administration, and then help to define the deliverables and/or outcomes. • Engage in modified consensus to reach decisions. *Modified consensus* means that everyone is heard but recognizes that often decisions do not have 100% agreement. • Sometimes innovative ideas may not come from academic sources (e.g., they may come from the finance office), and faculty can feel defensive. Invite ideas from staff and build on them. • Innovation needs champions and cheerleaders. Find and cultivate them for each strategic process. • Help others to let go of perfectionism in strategic solutions. • Invite radical ideas from others.
STAFF	**Intrapersonal** • Staff often have longevity at institutions and are able to model how to be student-focused. How might you bring these strengths to create strategic directions within shared governance? • Staff often are quite involved in the daily operations. How might you bring these strengths to the operational tasks within shared governance? **Interpersonal** • Ask for a clearly framed charge from administration, and then help to define the deliverables and/or outcomes. • Engage in modified consensus to reach decisions. *Modified consensus* means that everyone is heard but recognizes that often decisions do not have 100% agreement. • Innovation needs champions and cheerleaders. Find and cultivate them for each strategic process. • Help others to let go of perfectionism in strategic solutions. • Invite radical ideas from others.

BOT	**Intrapersonal** • Typically, the Board of Trustees operates at the strategic level. Do you assume the tasks are operational, strategic, or both? How do you know when either is necessary? • Universities need to be fiscally viable yet are different from a business. Reflect on the similarities and differences. • Often, an alumni trustee will have a nostalgic vision of the institution, based on their historical and personal experiences. Update your understanding of the realities for current students. **Interpersonal** • Shared governance works better when the BOT is less operational. Try to stay focused on the big picture and help others to do so as well. • Engage in modified consensus to reach decisions. *Modified consensus* means that everyone is heard but recognizes that often decisions do not have 100% agreement. • Innovation needs champions and cheerleaders. Find and cultivate them for each strategic process. • Help others to let go of perfectionism in strategic solutions. • Invite radical ideas from others.
STUDENTS	**Intrapersonal** • Your time at the institution may be over before strategic initiatives are implemented. How might you think beyond your own current needs to those of future generations of students? **Interpersonal** • Ask for a clearly framed charge from administration, and then help to define the deliverables and/or outcomes. • Engage in modified consensus to reach decisions. *Modified consensus* means that everyone is heard but recognizes that often decisions do not have 100% agreement. • Innovation needs champions and cheerleaders. Find and cultivate them for each strategic process. • Help others to let go of perfectionism in strategic solutions. • Invite radical ideas from others.

To explore this chapter's ideas further, consider the following questions related to the shared governance process.

1. Notice your own preference for operational or strategic discussions and processes. Do you like to focus more on a specific, defined issue? Or do you need to see the big picture? Are you more excited by discussion of the overall direction?

2. Reflect on your assumptions about shared governance committee work—overall, and from the perspective of your role. Do you assume the tasks are operational, strategic, or both? How do you know when either is necessary?

ACTIVITIES

---

1. Make a list of all the standing committees at your institution. How many of them have an operational focus? Which, if any, focus on strategic directions?

CHAPTER FIVE: COMMUNICATION

"The single biggest problem in communication is the illusion that it has taken place."
— George Bernard Shaw

TOPICS COVERED IN THIS CHAPTER:

- Effective communication within and across groups

- Defining transparency and sharing data broadly to improve communication

Overview

To choreograph a beautiful and complex Tango, the dance partners need to communicate in a variety of ways. Sometimes, the steps will be written down on paper to visualize and learn prior to any physical movement. Reviewing videos of other dancers may help the partners to see what the finished dance can look like. At times during the dance itself, the communication can be a subtle touch of a hand on the back, or a shift in posture. The dance experience is elevated for both the dancers themselves and the audience when the communication works well: when steps flow, the dance looks effortless, and the movement is joyful. If the reverse occurs and the communication is poor, toes may be stepped on and the dance may appear awkward and disjointed.

Similarly, during shared governance processes, communication continually takes place. Just as with the Tango, the success of the shared governance process depends on the effectiveness of the communication within it. As we considered this chapter, we noted that sometimes communication is required among the 'dancers' (that is, the people on the committee or in the meeting itself), while at other times, the communication needs to be directed toward the 'audience' (as when representatives share with their constituent groups or when administrative leaders provide institution-wide updates). Before we examine these two levels of communication that need to occur, we need to address the most important communication issue of all: communicating the definition of shared governance itself.

> ### DEFINING SHARED GOVERNANCE
>
> In Chapter One, we discussed the importance of establishing an agreed-upon definition of shared governance and of examining the various assumptions that each constituency may hold about it. As a foundation to all communication related to shared governance processes, we encourage institutions and the various shared governance structures to read and discuss the AAUP Red Book.[3] Through these discussions, constituencies can develop a definition that works for their institution and can be referred to as needed. The process of developing this definition will, itself, strengthen shared governance and build relationships.
>
> We believe it works well for these discussions to occur routinely and regularly, rather than in response to a crisis. Imagine how shared governance processes might be more effective if this discussion was held as part of the semester opening each year, to reaffirm and/or modify how the institutional constituencies want to work together in the upcoming academic year.

What Effective Communication and Transparency Look Like

Omnidirectional communication

How communication and transparency are defined by an institution can also impact effectiveness. Many times, communication is viewed as unidirectional: the expectation that administrators need to provide information to faculty, staff, and students. Rather, effective communication is *omni-directional* both among constituencies and within each constituency:

- *Within* each constituency, representatives need to provide and gather up-to-date information from their constituency membership.

- Communication *among* constituencies is often challenged by the concept of transparency and how it is defined. On almost all campuses, transparency is assumed to be the responsibility of administrators. Demands are made for institutional data to be shared by administrators with faculty and staff, yet faculty and staff balk at sharing the data of individual units or departments with each other.

Consider: What does it imply about trust and power dynamics at the institution if peers do not want others to see their data? As an institution discusses shared governance, this topic might be useful to explore as well, as an opportunity to discuss how to create radical transparency.

---

[3] See the AAUP Red Book at https://www.aaup.org/article/centennial-edition-aaup-redbook.

Meetings

Gathering people together to discuss issues is the ubiquitous process for shared governance. Sometimes the meetings are informal, taking place in a hallway or over lunch. Other times, meetings occur in committees or working groups, convening either remotely, in person, or both.

Committees often use Robert's Rules of Order to manage communication in meetings. Designed by U.S. Army officer Henry Martyn Robert, these Rules of Order create a structure to aid in discussion and decision making. This structure sometimes sacrifices a process to reach consensus, in service of maintaining orderly interactions. Equity-minded leaders may wish to look for other models that are less hierarchical, such as Martha's Rules, which are focused on consensus building.[4]

Whatever model you employ, here are a couple of general guidelines for increasing the effectiveness of committee and working group meetings:

- *All constituents should be represented and in the room for discussions and votes.* Leaders should be mindful that participation may vary based on who is remote or in person, and also because of power dynamics among constituencies. (See Chapter Two for more on power dynamics.) If everyone is not in the room, or if some in the room are not speaking, the decisions reached may not be communicated well to each constituency, or at all.

- *Each member of the group, and especially the leader facilitating the meeting, needs to listen to the use of 'they' or 'others' in the discussion.* If such terms are heard, such as "They need this," or "They will never agree," ask "Who is the 'they?'" Sometimes we hear people state "Other people won't like this." Ask, "Who are you referring to? Which others?" Use of this language can mean that the speaker themself holds the opinion they are speaking of, but that they want to attribute it to others. This might be an indication that there are unsafe power dynamics in the meeting. Or, it can mean that the speaker heard that opinion from one person, but they are making it sound as though they heard it from many people ("others"), so that the (often oppositional) view they are talking about appears bigger than it really is. Asking for clarification can help to discern the validity of the view by replacing a vague 'they' or 'other people' with specific context.

Communicating processes and decisions to the campus

Shared governance initiatives and their processes need to be communicated to the entire campus—as they emerge, during the proceedings of meetings, and once decisions are made. One of the most common complaints regarding shared governance decisions centers is that people have not been kept informed. Sometimes, that lack of awareness is due to poor communication within the constituency. That is, the representatives of that

---

[4]Minahan, Anne, "'Martha's Rules': An Alternative to Robert's Rules of Order" (1986). Sociology Department, Faculty Publications. 812. https://digitalcommons.unl.edu/sociologyfacpub/812

constituency who are involved in the shared governance process do not do a sufficient job of letting their people know what is underway. Other times, the lack of awareness is due to limited communication from administration.

Two common mistakes are using an effective modality or only communicating once about a complex issue. Communications about less substantive issues often happen via standing or codified shared governance processes—such as via minutes or reports. Ask yourself, "Who is likely to read these?" Decisions buried in reports or minutes may not reach people who are impacted.

Communications about complex decisions, or decisions that will result in a substantive change, need to be made often, and via various methods. When engaging in a substantive change, initial communications to the entire community might include information such as:

- The rationale for the initiative

- The timeline

- The committee members

- The process

Communication about the process needs to include the following:

- The plans for ongoing communication, such as the number and frequency of 'town halls' to discuss the topic, and how people can have input as a member of their constituency group.

- Who has the decision-making authority (see our discussion of decision-making authority in Chapters One and Seven; typically, the person who can be fired for a poor decision is the one who holds the decision-making authority).

Writing an effective charge to the committee is an important part of the communication to the working group. (See *Appendix: Writing an Effective Charge* at the end of this book for a template.) The more complex an issue, the more important it is to have multiple conversations with the various constituencies, to allow for questions and discussion. Follow-up communications during the process help to maximize involvement. Examples could include sharing videos for those who couldn't attend and sharing a written synopsis of the discussion to the entire campus community.

The type and size of the institution greatly impacts communication. Larger institutions, with their inherent complexity, can be challenged in their ability to reach all members of the community. They may also have more resources, such as a larger in-house communications unit to help manage communications. Smaller institutions may have built relationships that add a personalized aspect to communications.

In either case, omnidirectional communication does not need to be linear and sequential; it can and should take place concurrently. Discussing issues between and among constituencies, the working group or committee charged with the process, and administrative leaders can all occur at the same time. In fact, cross-fertilization of ideas can result in better consultation and in better decisions.

Institutions should make an investment to train constituency leadership and representatives about the importance of regular communication, and about how they can best communicate with and get input from their people. More experienced peers can help to provide their wisdom, and administration can create the opportunity for this training and discussion.

The Dance Steps

What each constituency needs to know about communication and transparency

We offer the following guidelines for each constituency about possible assumptions or actions that can help or harm the shared governance process. Remember, you can use these steps in your current role and *also* to help understand the perspectives of others with whom you are working to create effective shared governance.

As you identify assumptions during your shared governance processes—both your own assumptions and others'—making these explicit can help to examine them. If these assumptions are operating, they are important to note so that they can be questioned if they are inaccurate or embedded into the process if they are accurate.

DANCE STEPS: COMMUNICATION
ADMINISTRATORS
Intrapersonal
• Administrators have disproportionately more responsibility to build relationships and assure that communication is effective.
• Our personal style affects communication and how relationships are built. Consider whether you are more of an *extrovert* (you get energy from interactions with lots of people) or *introvert* (you get energy from the inner world of ideas). If you identify as the former, you may gravitate toward communicating via larger, in-person events. If you identify with the latter, it may feel more difficult to engage in those types of events, and you may prefer written communications. In both cases, push yourself to communicate in ways that are beyond your comfort zone.
Interpersonal
• Include representatives, as much as possible, at your regular meetings within your unit. Trust that they can keep items confidential if needed.

ADMINISTRATORS

- Effective communication necessitates an iterative process. Communicate about shared governance issues many times over many modalities.

- Communicate any changes in the process as early as possible. Surprises can derail the process and undermine trust.

- Communication plans should consider the sequencing of approvals, and how the constituency's participation builds on the decision made by the next level. (unit/dept → college → univ → BOT).

- Consider the use of focus groups to increase involvement.

- Reaching all constituencies directly and concurrently is mandatory. Rumors multiply otherwise.

- We each have been trained to write from a distinct disciplinary style. Most others at the institution have not been trained in your discipline. Use clear and professional communication that is not specific to your discipline.

- Data should be shared and updated. While data is necessary, however, sharing *just* the data is not sufficient. Also share the assumptions used to produce it. Put data in context and acknowledge where there are gaps. Consider that data may be both quantitative and qualitative, and both are valuable.

- Communication about shared governance issues must occur within the president's cabinet.

  - If you oversee a unit (e.g., VP over a division), the process may occur entirely within your area. As a courtesy, be sure to keep other administrators informed, however. While this is not mandated as part of shared governance, decisions in your area may have unintended consequences for others.

  - If you are in the role of president or chancellor, it is vital that you back up other administrators when they are making hard decisions within shared governance.

FACULTY

Intrapersonal

- Our personal style affects communication and how relationships are built. Consider whether you are more of an *extrovert* (you get energy from interactions with lots of people) or *introvert* (you get energy from the inner world of ideas). If you identify as the former, you may gravitate toward communicating via larger, in-person events. If you identify with the latter, it may feel more difficult to engage in those types of events, and you may prefer written communications. In both cases, push yourself to communicate in ways that are beyond your comfort zone.

- Faculty are trained to investigate and try to answer *why*. While this is valuable in our disciplines, it does not always serve shared governance well. Issues are often complex, and there are multiple causes or needs. Monitor your need to know *why*. Some investigative questions are useful; however, do not let your desire to investigate stall the process unnecessarily. Know when to stop asking *why* and instead focus on the issue to be resolved, and move forward.

FACULTY	**Interpersonal** • If you are serving in a role that represents a group of faculty for shared governance, be sure to communicate with those you represent to get a broad view of their ideas. Reach out to your constituency often. • Get involved from the beginning. You will develop a more complex understanding of the issues. Ideas from those who are involved from the beginning tend to be more respected. • If part of the faculty leadership, your voice is an equal partner to the provost's in representing academics. • Try to engage within the agreed-upon shared governance processes. Only circumvent processes and structures (taking actions such as going directly to the president or the Board of Trustees) in *extreme* circumstances.
STAFF	**Intrapersonal** • Our personal style affects communication and how relationships are built. Consider whether you are more of an *extrovert* (you get energy from interactions with lots of people) or *introvert* (you get energy from the inner world of ideas). If you identify as the former, you may gravitate toward communicating via larger, in-person events. If you identify with the latter, it may feel more difficult to engage in those types of events, and you may prefer written communications. In both cases, push yourself to communicate in ways that are beyond your comfort zone. **Interpersonal** • If you are serving in a role that represents a group of staff for shared governance, be sure to communicate with those you represent to get a broad view of their ideas. Reach out to your constituency often. • Get involved from the beginning. You will develop a more complex understanding of the issues. Ideas from those who are involved from the beginning tend to be more respected. • If you are part of the staff leadership, your voice is an equal partner to the vice president in representing your area. • Try to engage within the agreed-upon shared governance processes. Only circumvent processes and structures (taking actions such as going directly to the president or the Board of Trustees) in *extreme* circumstances.

BOT	**Intrapersonal** • Our personal style affects communication and how relationships are built. Consider whether you are more of an *extrovert* (you get energy from interactions with lots of people) or *introvert* (you get energy from the inner world of ideas). If you identify as the former, you may gravitate toward communicating via larger, in-person events. If you identify with the latter, it may feel more difficult to engage in those types of events, and you may prefer written communications. In both cases, push yourself to communicate in ways that are beyond your comfort zone. • Since your role holds a great deal of control and power, monitor your inclination to present your views first. Be sure to make room for others to speak. **Interpersonal** • In your role, you have a lot of power and control, and you are making decisions that impact many people. This makes it very important to communicate with and listen to faculty, staff, and student voices who will be impacted by your decisions. • Make room to hear these voices directly by judiciously opening some meeting time for all to attend.
STUDENTS	**Intrapersonal** • Our personal style affects communication and how relationships are built. Consider whether you are more of an *extrovert* (you get energy from interactions with lots of people) or *introvert* (you get energy from the inner world of ideas). If you identify as the former, you may gravitate toward communicating via larger, in-person events. If you identify with the latter, it may feel more difficult to engage in those types of events, and you may prefer written communications. In both cases, push yourself to communicate in ways that are beyond your comfort zone. **Interpersonal** • You are likely serving in a role that represents a group of students for shared governance, so be sure to communicate with those you represent to get a broad view of their ideas. Reach out to your constituency often. • Get involved from the beginning. You will develop a more complex understanding of the issues. Ideas from those who are involved from the beginning tend to be more respected. • Try to engage within the agreed-upon shared governance processes. Only circumvent processes and structures (taking actions such as going directly to the president or the Board of Trustees) in *extreme* circumstances.

To explore this chapter's ideas further, consider the following questions related to the shared governance process.

1. What is the definition of shared governance at your institution? If you have a ready answer, is the definition agreed to across constituencies? How do you know? If you don't have a ready answer, how might you think about introducing the idea to discuss and develop a shared definition to others on your campus?

2. What data are transparent at your institution? What data are not? What might be the impact of this on shared governance?

3. Think about times when you were able to effectively communicate a decision. What did you do? How did you know your communication was effective?

4. Do you think of yourself as an introvert or an extrovert? How does this preference impact your communication style? What types of communication do you rely on, and which might you need to strengthen?

CHAPTER SIX:
URGENCY (TEMPO)

"It's always about timing. If it's too soon, no one understands. If it's too late, everyone's forgotten."
— Anna Wintour

> TOPICS COVERED IN THIS CHAPTER:
>
> • Factors that impact timing of shared governance processes
>
> • How a sense of urgency impacts shared governance

What is the Right Tempo?

An effective Tango requires the dancers to be in sync, finding the right tempo so that the steps can appear naturally graceful and beautiful. Too slow, and the dance will appear to be an effort; too fast, and it will be difficult to follow and fully appreciate.

Shared governance also requires finding the 'right' tempo and timing. The processes must allow adequate time for articulating the purpose and task at hand, gathering data including consultation, and a timeline for a decision and implementation. "Adequate," however, might have different meanings for different constituencies and about different issues.

The risks of moving too slow or too fast

Acting too quickly or too slowly can create harm either way:

- Sometimes, we need more time than the circumstances allow. Mandates from external forces—legislatures, changing demographics, students and their family demands—all can conspire to create pressure to act quickly, sometimes too hastily.

- Other times, the shared governance processes themselves slow movement to a crawl, and we miss opportunities.

- A third possibility is that, at some institutions, shared governance may be the tool that is used to purposefully delay changes, or to sideline them indefinitely. This creates the illusion of support, when in fact there is none.

One of us worked on a campus where the provost had a unique use of tempo. They would sit back while the shared governance processes unfolded, which on this particular campus were quite robust. Even seemingly minor matters would take a long time, involving multiple iterations and multiple votes. Once the process concluded and reached the provost's desk for approval, they did not quickly sign off. During the interim time period, the campus assumed the outcome was a fait accompli and acted like it was an official policy. Only after it was assumed (and later embraced) as the 'way things are done' did the provost sign the policy and make it official.

Which issues to bring up when

The tempo of shared governance can involve more than just the timing of the process itself. The timing of *which issues to bring up when* is also crucial. Engaging only in low-stakes issues can lower morale, as this can imply to some constituencies that their input is not important. Issues with larger impact can increase involvement, although too many big changes at the same time can exhaust all constituencies. Many of us recall the COVID-19 pandemic fatigue that occurred during the height of the pandemic, in which institutions had to quickly and frequently use shared governance to react to the pandemic. Once the pandemic waned, many constituencies were exhausted.

Speeding up the tempo in a crisis

However, COVID-19 also increased the speed by which shared governance processes occurred, often far more quickly than higher education had ever experienced before. Yet even with this unprecedented speed and urgency, many of these processes worked well. From this, many institutions learned that shared governance does not have to move as slowly as it does by default.

_____

*The question now is: How can institutions speed up shared governance processes,
when necessary, without a deadly pandemic to motivate this speed?*

_____

There are other crises that can motivate such innovation. For example, enrollment drops constitute an epidemic for many geographic areas in the U.S., one that may impact the financial health of an institution. Delays can be deadly for the financial health of an institution, yet if shared governance processes are able to move quickly in this context, decisions about closing existing programs or starting new academic programs can help an institution survive.

The tempo needs to consider the impact on the equity and inclusion

Also, the pace of the process needs to include time to consider the decision's probable impact on people of all identities, in the interest of equity and inclusion. Processes need to include questions that address the impact of the initiative or policy change on all groups.

We need to ask about each decision, "Who will this benefit? Who might it harm?"

When considering the impact of a decision on the campus community, we need consider people of all ethnicities, genders, ages, class statuses, and other positionality within the institution. It may take time to gather the necessary data and input to achieve a decision that does not inadvertently advantage some groups of people over others.

The tempo needs to consider the finality of the decision

The tempo of the process can be moderated by the finality of the decision. Sometimes, an institution has more of an appetite for change if the constituents view the changes as a pilot. Piloting significant changes within a limited scope allows some time to test innovations or disruptions to current practice, including the impact on various groups. It allows institutions to measure outcomes and use them to keep what works and make modifications as needed. Using a pilot approach challenges the assumption that we need 'perfection' before moving forward; it also is good practice that allows for and encourages learning from doing, and continuous improvement.

The tempo needs to consider the boundaries of the academic calendar

Lastly, we would be remiss if we did not briefly mention the reality of semester boundaries and their impacts on the tempo of shared governance. At many institutions, shared governance exists within the reality of the rhythm of semesters, as well as faculty nine-month contract periods. Add in winter breaks and the busyness of the ends of semesters due to finals or commencements, and notice how all of these conditions create a realistic window of maybe seven to eight months in which to engage in effective shared governance processes. Big decisions made over the summer are almost always viewed with suspicion, even if the process was conducted well.

Semester rhythms can be used to help with making decisions more quickly or they can slow decisions down. The impacts of semesters should be considered based on the issues under consideration. For example, using the academic year rhythm can help when creating a charge for a task force or a committee:

- The end date for the task at hand can be used to create urgency, if needed.

- On the other hand, starting a process in the spring semester will almost always create a multiple-year process.

You may need to plan backward from the date when the decision needs to go into effect and start the process accordingly. In doing this, consider all constituents who will be providing consultation.

Let's imagine you want to implement new promotion and tenure processes starting for the next cycle in the fall. Given the need for the various faculty shared-governance structures to weigh in—such as the promotion and tenure committee, and the faculty senate—as well as the need for institutional policy committee(s) and/or officials to 'sign off,' does starting with the previous fall allow sufficient time? Will the 7-8 months of lead time be enough?

Finding the 'right' tempo for a shared governance process is an art. The simplicity or the complexity of the task may allow you to speed up or necessitate slowing down. Just as with the Tango, too slow will ruin the experience of the dancers and the audience. Too fast, and the dancers will trip over themselves, and the audience won't be able to follow along.

The Dance Steps

What each constituency needs to know about shared governance in relation to timelines

We offer the following guidelines for each constituency about the effects on timelines and the sense of urgency, or lack thereof. Remember, you can use these steps in your current role and *also* to help understand the perspectives of others with whom you are working to create effective shared governance.

Notice and question your own sense of urgency, or lack of urgency, as you engage in various shared governance processes. Lastly, specifically question the impact of moving either too quickly or too slowly. As you question your sense of urgency or lack of urgency, ask how does it serve the students? Yourself? Your colleagues? The institution?

DANCE STEPS: TEMPO

ADMINISTRATORS

Intrapersonal

- Question your own sense of urgency, especially when you want initiatives to move quickly.

- Take time to consider unintended effects on all populations—by gender, ethnicity, class status, age, (dis)ability, and other marginalized identities.

- Slower movement through the shared governance process is often frustrating to administrators. Examine reasons for your frustration.

Interpersonal

- If there is necessary urgency to the shared governance process, consider how concurrent conversations and consultations can help with quickening the timeline.

- Attend to the rhythms of the academic year. Try to avoid decisions regarding major changes during times when others, especially faculty, are off-contract or off campus.

- The rhythm of the academic year may also dictate the timeline you establish in the 'charge' regarding the task at hand.

- Note the frustration that some administrators feel for slow-moving processes mentioned above. If the slow movement negatively impacts students or a marginalized identity group, share that impact with others who might be moving more slowly.

- Sometimes those in administration might use the slower process of shared governance on purpose. If the initiative impacts many constituents or the financial health of the institution, slowing down the shared governance process might be beneficial.

- The Board of Trustees often wants quick action and sometimes does not understand how shared governance works. Educate your BOT about shared governance and their role; yet sometimes this is not enough. Learn when and how to 'stall' their need for urgent decisions if that will detail effective shared governance processes and undermine trust.

FACULTY

Intrapersonal

- Question your own sense of urgency, especially when you want initiatives to move slowly.

- When you want initiatives to move slowly, ask what part of your lack of urgency may be a general resistance to change or a misplaced need for perfection. Consider these along with the need to move slowly to make sure that the process has included adequate consultation and that various impacts have been considered.

FACULTY	• Notice which initiatives you might want quicker action on, such as those that might benefit faculty directly—like negotiation about salary raises.
	• Take time to consider the unintended effects of moving slowly or quickly on students and/or colleagues, and by gender, ethnicity, class status, age, (dis)ability, and other marginalized identities.
	Interpersonal
	• Work with colleagues to provide timely consultation and/or decision making.
	• If other constituents seem to be acting with an urgency you don't feel, ask them to explain the consequences of moving too slowly. Sometimes in the context of shared governance in higher education, opportunities for success are increased if the process can be done both well and quickly.
	• Consider if the urgency of any particular initiative/issue warrants shared governance participation outside of your contract period, such as during the summer. Sometimes the best-planned timelines shift and need faculty input during summer.
STAFF	**Intrapersonal**
	• Question your own sense of urgency, especially when you want initiatives to move slowly.
	• When you want initiatives to move slowly, ask what part of your lack of urgency may be a general resistance to change or a misplaced need for perfection. Consider these along with the need to move slowly to make sure that the process has included adequate consultation and that various impacts have been considered.
	• Notice which initiatives you might want quicker action on, such as those that might benefit faculty directly—like negotiation about salary raises.
	• Take time to consider the unintended effects of moving slowly or quickly on student and/or colleagues, and by gender, ethnicity, class status, age, (dis)ability, and other marginalized identities.
	Interpersonal
	• Work with colleagues to provide timely consultation and/or decision making.
	• If other constituents seem to be acting with an urgency you don't feel, ask them to explain the consequences of moving too slowly. Sometimes in the context of shared governance in higher education, opportunities for success are increased if the process can be done both well and quickly.

BOT	• Be attentive to how urgency in shared governance may leave out your constituency. Find allies among administrators and faculty who will advocate for staff, especially if the process is moving quickly. Conversely, if the process is moving slowly, use your voice to help others understand the impact on staff.
	Intrapersonal • Question your own sense of urgency, especially when you want initiatives to move quickly. • Take time to consider unintended effects on all populations, by gender, ethnicity, class status, age, (dis)ability, and other marginalized identities. • Slower movement through the shared governance process is often frustrating to members of a board. Examine reasons for your frustration. • If your work experience is not within higher education, it is important that you take time to learn the realities of an academic calendar on the workflow.
	Interpersonal • Many boards desire quick actions. Work with administration to craft the message as to why it's important. • Listen to the administrators and trust their judgments. Sometimes they will need to slow down a shared governance process, to assure trust and time for consultation. Remember that your role is strategic, not operational. • If you are mandating institutional changes that need the shared governance process, provide timelines that allow for both effective shared governance and achieve the desired changes to reach your intended institutional goals.
STUDENTS	**Intrapersonal** • Take time to consider unintended effects on all populations, by gender, ethnicity, class status, age, (dis)ability, and other marginalized identities.
	Interpersonal • Actively participate in shared governance by attending meetings and providing timely input.

To explore this chapter's ideas further, consider the following questions related to the shared governance process.

1. Consider the balance between urgency, data gathering, consultation, strategic vs. operational issues, and the effects on the institution. Which issues might necessitate a quicker process? Which might benefit from slowing down?

2. Has your institution ever implemented changes via a pilot project? How did that impact the ability to make changes? Once no longer a pilot, did the project/actions continue and if so, which changes were made for continuous improvement?

3. Note any expectations you hold about perfection before agreeing to try something new. Can you approach your shared governance decisions with a 'good enough' mindset, knowing that most everything can be changed again?

4. Consider what helped to create effective shared governance processes during the COVID-19 pandemic at your institution. How can you replicate these aspects for other urgent matters?

5. Consider what did not work well or did not engage shared governance effectively during the COVID-19 pandemic. What would you want to avoid for future urgent matters?

CHAPTER SEVEN:
CONCLUSION—CREATING THE DANCE

---

*"If art is the bridge between what you see in your mind and what the world sees,
then skill is how you build that bridge." – Twyla Tharp*

TOPICS COVERED IN THIS CHAPTER:

- Clarifying roles in decision making (with a matrix template)

- Evaluation and continuous improvement of shared governance

Clarifying Roles in Decision Making

Just as the distinctiveness of the Tango can be attributed having roots in multiple African and European cultures, the practice of shared governance on each campus depends on the melding of perspectives and the roles played by multiple parties. As stated in Chapters One and Two, the crux of the power dynamic of shared governance is how to empower and collaborate—listen and consult—*and* make decisions. How these dynamics play out is dependent on all parties keeping an agreed-upon definition of shared governance, and its components, top of mind. Specifically, who does what—and when.

CLARIFY AND DEFINE:

- Who approves
- Who consults
- Who decides
- Who informs
- Who recommends

On the next page, you will find the template for a matrix that can be used to help constituency groups clarify roles and responsibilities when considering institutional policies and procedures. The first row of the template is completed as an example. We encourage each campus to fill out this chart, collaboratively, with all constituencies. The end result will be useful, and the process will help to clear up misconceptions before a complex decision needs to be reached.

SHARED GOVERNANCE ROLES AND RESPONSIBILITIES MATRIX (WITH EXAMPLE)					
	APPROVES	**CONSULTS**	**DECIDES**	**INFORMS**	**RECOMMENDS**
Academic Policies (proposed by faculty senate)	President/ Chancellor	Student senate Staff senate Academic deans	Faculty senate	Board	Provost Academic deans
Business Processes					
Curricular Matters					
Enrollment Management Policies					
Fiscal Affairs					
HR Policies (non-academic)					
HR Policies (academic)					
Strategic Planning					

SHARED GOVERNANCE ROLES AND RESPONSIBILITIES MATRIX (BLANK TEMPLATE)					
	APPROVES	**CONSULTS**	**DECIDES**	**INFORMS**	**RECOMMENDS**
Academic Policies (proposed by faculty senate)					
Business Processes					
Curricular Matters					
Enrollment Management Policies					
Fiscal Affairs					
HR Policies (non-academic)					
HR Policies (academic)					
Strategic Planning					

If this matrix feels too restrictive...

Some campuses may find the roles and responsibilities matrix approach too structured and restrictive—not flexible enough to accommodate situations that require complete confidentiality or unexpected situations, such as the 2020 lockdown forced by COVID-19 or by natural disasters. For those who opt *not* to use this matrixed approach, near-continuous omnidirectional communication will be required to clarify the "who does what, when" question. If this is the case, the trust matrix in Chapter One may be useful. For institutions who have developed or plan to develop a roles and responsibilities matrix, the trust matrix may prove useful when navigating uncharted shared governance territory.

Evaluation and Improvement of Shared Governance

The closing topic of this book is the evaluation and continuous improvement of shared governance. When interviewing faculty, staff, students, and administrators to gather information for this book, there was only a passing mention of evaluating and improving shared governance. Most people with whom we spoke were so consumed with tackling their campuses' grand challenges that they pushed aside reflection on what might or might not be working.

We surmise that the neglect of evaluation and continuous improvement efforts may be at least partially responsible for the reports we heard of failing shared governance: disengaged constituency group leaders, unproductive meetings, moribund committees, and dysfunctional governance bodies.

We recommend instituting formal and informal methods of assessing shared governance.

Formal methods

The AAUP Shared Governance Assessment Tool can be used as-is, or modified to meet the specific needs of an institution.[5] The Association of Governing Boards of Universities and Colleges (AGB.org) also provides resources for assessing the effectiveness of shared governance. Campus leaders may seek information from other institutions in search of assessment practices to consider. For example, SUNY Voices[6], the moniker for shared governance for the State University of New York System, is a rich source of information, including publications and a *Campus Governance Leaders Toolkit*.[7]

---

[5]See https://www.aaup.org/sites/default/files/AAUP_Shared_Governance_Assessment_Tool.pdf
[6]See https://www.suny.edu/about/shared-governance/sunyvoices/
[7]See https://www.suny.edu/about/shared-governance/sunyvoices/cgl-toolkit/

Formal evaluations, such as surveys, should take place at regular intervals and involve all stakeholder groups. Findings should be widely shared with the aim of developing improvement plans.

Informal methods

The parties involved in the Tango, just like shared governance, must practice often; otherwise, the participants will be too out of shape to be effective. Less formal and more frequent means of assessing shared governance can be instituted by any consistency group at any point in time by checking "vital signs." Just as the vital signs for the human body are body temperature, blood pressure, and pulse, the vital signs for shared governance are *engagement*, *communication/transparency*, and *outcomes*. Quick shared governance checks should be a self-assessment— a way to take responsibility for the group's role in healthy or unhealthy shared governance.

Self-diagnostic questions can be as simple and uncomplicated as the following:

CHECKING VITAL SIGNS

- **Engagement:** In what ways are we engaged or disengaged in shared governance? Are there ways to be more engaged in shared governance?

- **Communication/Transparency:** What is working well in shared governance communication? Where are the opportunities for us to improve communication and transparency between and among constituency groups? How do our assumptions/perspectives impact our ability to communicate effectively between and among constituency groups?

- **Outcomes:** Are we reaching most of our desired outcomes? In what ways are we falling short of achieving the desired outcomes of shared governance processes?

No need to create a lengthy instrument. These questions can be included on a meeting agenda a few times during the academic year to seed discussion and recommit to organizational learning that results in healthy shared governance and in the success of the institution and its students.

Concluding Remarks

No one learns a complex dance like the Tango in just one rehearsal session. Each step needs to be practiced before it can be combined into the beautiful movements performed by experienced dancers.

Shared governance is similar. Each of us needs to rehearse, step by step. In fact, we may need to start with unlearning some habits, like the assumptions about conflict and mal-intent discussed in Chapter One. We might need to spend some time thinking through our role, decision making, and consultation. We may need to consider how to improve our use of the structures and communication modalities within shared governance. Finally, we may need to infuse methods to help our decision making in shared governance to be as equitable and inclusive as possible.

Shared governance was designed with the hope of challenging hierarchal, uninformed decisions. It was designed to respect and include the perspectives brought by each constituency. We hope the ideas presented in this book, the tips provided, and the reflections you make for yourself will help you to rehearse and practice the steps. As you do this, for yourself and with others, shared governance at your institution will become a more enjoyable experience for all who participate. Pick your partner(s) and dance!

PART TWO:
CASE STUDIES

CASE STUDIES

In this section, we have provided case studies that can help you explore the ideas presented in this workbook. They address various issues that may arise in a shared governance environment. We hope you will use these as a catalyst for discussion at your institution. Using these as low-stakes activities can help to build relationships, uncover assumptions, build some shared understandings, and aid in communications among constituencies. Enjoy!

Introducing Jackson Rockgrove University: Mission, Values, and Characters

The case studies that follow are set at the fictional Jackson Rockgrove University. Before you embark on these activities, here is a quick introduction to the institution and its community. Refer back to this section as needed, as you complete and discuss the case studies.

JRU MISSION

- We develop responsible citizens and leaders through inclusive educational opportunities.

JRU VALUES

- Excellence
- Diversity
- Community engagement
- Global perspective
- Service
- Sustainability

Case study characters

BIG BUCKS BENTLEY. Donor/alum/trustee. Has multiple endowments at the institution; MBA from the institution; owns a large regional company.

PROFESSOR COMBATIVE. Has a very limited and poor scholarship record, with marginal teaching performance. Hired six years ago.

DR. DISSATISFIED. Tenured, associate professor; at the institution for 25 years. Never elected to leadership or appointed to interim administrative roles, even though they wanted these roles.

DR. DOGMA. Associate professor; worked at the institution for 25 years. Started as an adjunct, and earned doctorate eight years ago; newly tenured.

DREW DRAMA. Relative of Big Bucks Bentley; floating employee, has reported to six areas over ten years.

PROVOST EARNEST. In office for six months. Previously served long-term as a department chair and has been dean at two different institutions.

FINDLEY FIREBALL. A senior, Fireball is serving their second year as undergraduate Student Senate President.

FRANKIE FISCAL. Chief Financial Officer. At the institution for 15 years; newly promoted to CFO from within.

DR. HOPEWELL. Associate professor, and newly elected chair of a large department.

HARPER HUSTLE. A full professor in the science department.

DEAN LACKEY. Has been serving as a dean for approximately eight years. Dean Lackey's strategy for keeping their job is to maintain the goodwill of their college faculty at almost all costs.

MURPHY MEAGER. ABD (adjunct); has vacillated between temporary full-time and adjunct appointments for two years at the institution. Has been working on their dissertation for five years.

PROFESSOR MENSCH. Associate professor, well-rounded campus citizen in teaching (excellent), scholarship, (prolific), service (does as asked).

DR. ABBY MONKSON. Senate President; associate professor, co-led program review process. Served on the Faculty Senate for 12 years; second term as Senate President.

NEWBY NELSON. Vice President of Student Success. Newby's purview includes student affairs, enrollment management, and advancement. They are new to the campus.

DEAN OUTSIDER. Second year in the role; served as dean at another institution before coming to this current position.

PROFESSOR PASSIONATE. Very limited, poor scholarship with marginal teaching performance. Hired six years ago.

DEAN PERFECT. Retired dean who previously presided over Dean Outsider's current college. Perfect has returned to faculty and keeps a low profile.

PRESIDENT PETRY. In office for three years; is very concerned with appearances and popularity; doesn't want to make anyone mad. Lives in fear of a vote of no confidence, especially based on campus racial climate issues.

DR. PAT POMPOUS. Department chair, associate professor, former Senate leader; co-led program review process; in an accredited program that allows for multiple releases for their administration time.

ROWAN REGISTRAR. Has worked in the registrar's office for 30 years, working their way up from receptionist to registrar. They have been registrar for the past 10 years.

COACH SOUTHPAW SANDERS. Baseball coach and former pitcher for the L.A. Dodgers. Promoted a year ago to Athletic Director after retirement of the previous AD.

PROFESSOR SINGER. MFA, associate professor, tenured; in their third term as chair of the music department.

SLOAN SOLO. Joined JRU as the Chief Diversity Officer two years ago. The office consists of Sloan and a part-time graduate assistant.

SYDNEY SPOKESPERSON. Public Relations and Communications Director. Sydney has presidential ambitions.

STEVIE STAFF. Comptroller, reports to Frankie Fiscal. President of Staff Senate for several terms.

TANNER TRUE. Associate Provost. Well-respected, former chair of the science department for many years, recently hired to serve in this role after a national search.

MONA VOLADOR. Human Resources Director and Title IX Director. Has spent their career at this institution, starting at Secretary. Promoted to the role rather than selected through a search process. Does not have any formal education in HR. Their Title IX duties often extend to all Civil Rights EEOC potential issues.

DR. WAVERLY ROCKEFELLER WARBUCKS. Recently tenured associate professor. Both parents were professors at JRU.

DEAN WINK. Was promoted from within about three years ago after serving as a chair of a very successful prestigious department. Has a history of being very friendly and flirty with colleagues.

JACKSON ROCKGROVE UNIVERSITY ORG CHART

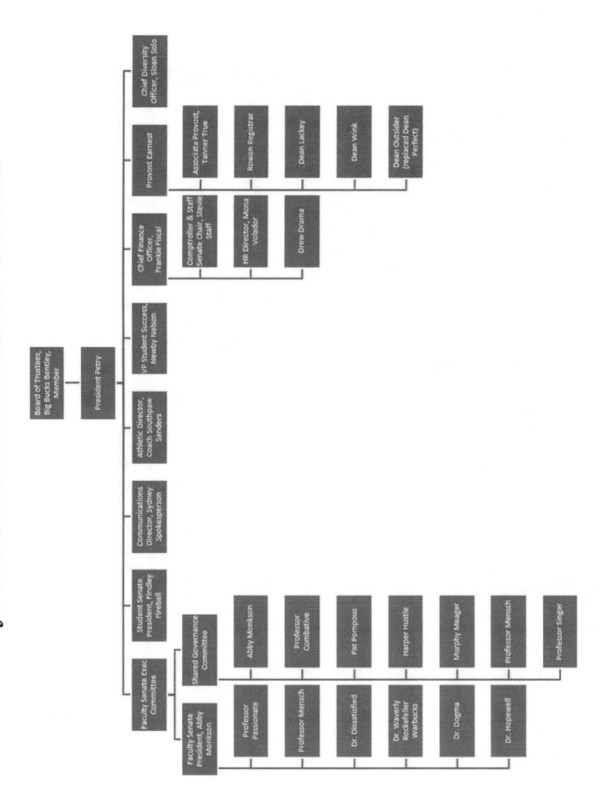

The Case Studies

CASE STUDY #1: THE CASE OF THE DICKENSIAN DEPARTMENTS

Early in their tenure, Provost Earnest would repeatedly hear snarky comments regarding the colossal size of the budget in the office of the provost at any meeting where resource allocation was mentioned. Dr. Dogma would make long, impassioned statements at senate meetings railing against the heinous imbalance of funding, likening academic departments to the impoverished characters in a Dickens novel. Dogma was praised and admired by faculty colleagues for having the courage to speak truth to power.

Knowing that the statements about the budget were not true, Earnest decides to email the entire academic affairs budget—with spending details—to every person working in the division. This unexpected move results in shock and anger among the faculty. In reality, the provost's office had only 10% of the academic affairs budget, and some of the largest budgets were in the departments with the fewest students (including Dr. Dogma's department). Once the myth was dispelled, a major plank was removed from Dr. Dogma's platform as the self-appointed moral center of the campus, and they did not speak during the remaining senate meetings for the semester.

After the public release of the budget, Provost Earnest developed a new budget model that more closely aligned with enrollment in each department, and there was very little pushback. The only people who openly complained were faculty in units where the budgets were disproportionately large compared to the number of students they served—an inequity enabled by the lack of transparency and the acceptance of rumor as truth. In the end, a few people stepped down from the moral high ground and humbly but privately apologized to the Provost, admitting that they had never asked for nor seen any budget figures, but had blindly accepted and spread the rumor.

As you explore this case study, consider the following:

CONSIDER:

1. What trust issues are implied or evident in this case study?

2. What intentions might be held by each person involved? By each department of faculty?

3. What purpose(s) did the budget myth serve? Why would faculty not request to see the budget, given the rumor of the gross funding imbalance?

4. Unexpectedly releasing the budget was a guerilla tactic. Given that the rumor was widely accepted, was this the best or only way the Provost could squash it? What other actions might the Provost have taken to share the truth about the budget? How did the action impact trust between administration and faculty?

5. As you read the case study, did you have an image for each character? If so, what gender and ethnicity did you imagine? (This might help you uncover some implicit bias.)

   Now consider the almost infinite possibilities of people's identities in the case study, and the shifting power dynamics:

   a. Gender: If you imagined a character as either male or female, try switching your image to another gender, including non-binary.

   b. Ethnicity: If you imagined a character as a particular ethnicity, try switching your image to another ethnicity.

   c. Intersectional identities: Imagine different permutations of interactions between people of varying intersecting identities. (For example, imagine the case study with all White men, all White women, all African American men, all African American women, all men of color of different ethnicities, all women of color of different ethnicities, mixed genders of the same ethnicity, mixed genders across ethnicities.)

   As you imagine different identities, consider the potential effects on interactions.

   Would your answers or suggestions to any of the questions asked above change, given shifting power dynamics, across all of these intersecting permutations?

Case Study #2: The Case of the Provost by Checklist

Under President Petry, the composition and power dynamics of the administration have shifted dramatically. Under their leadership, multiple assistant vice president positions have been created, and when administrators leave, they are often appointed or placed in an interim role without shared governance input or process. The institution now has only two academic deans, Wink and Lackey, and the former is an appointed interim.

Last year, it was announced that Provost Earnest was going 'on leave,' and that President Petry would now serve as Acting Chief Academic Officer, with input from the two remaining deans. Just last week, President Petry shared the process to request for new or replacement faculty positions. A checklist of all criteria was provided; departments were to fill this out and send it to the CFO, Frankie Fiscal, for funding, if enough criteria were met. Faculty members Dissatisfied and Combative were appalled that there was no academic strategic vision and/or administrative role overseeing these requests. The deans were glad that they were not being held accountable for making any of these hard and likely contentious decisions.

CONSIDER:

1. What is the typical role of each shared governance constituency in the approval of new/replacement positions? What might be the typical role of a provost?

2. As these decisions are made and/or consultation occurs, what balance should there be between institutional academic needs and institutional financial needs?

3. What options are available to Dissatisfied and Combative? What options within shared governance? And what options outside shared governance?

4. What process might have been designed instead, given the current administrative structure?

5. As you read the case study, did you have an image for each character? If so, what gender and ethnicity did you imagine? (This might help you uncover some implicit bias.)

    Now consider the almost infinite possibilities of people's identities in the case study, and the shifting power dynamics:

    a. Gender: If you imagined a character as either male or female, try switching your image to another gender, including non-binary.

    b. Ethnicity: If you imagined a character as a particular ethnicity, try switching your image to another ethnicity.

    c. Intersectional identities: Imagine different permutations of interactions between people of varying intersecting identities. (For example, imagine the case study with all White men, all White women, all African American men, all African American women, all men of color of different ethnicities, all women of color of different ethnicities, mixed genders of the same ethnicity, mixed genders across ethnicities.)

    As you imagine different identities, consider the potential effects on interactions.

    Would your answers or suggestions to any of the questions asked above change, given shifting power dynamics, across all of these intersecting permutations?

CASE STUDY #3: THE CASE OF "MONEY SPEAKS LOUDER"

Non-unionized, Jackson Rockgrove's shared governance included a compensation committee, composed of elected faculty representatives, Provost Earnest, and Frankie Fiscal, CFO. They would meet early in the spring semester, and their deliberations would continue until an agreement was reached. The faculty would bring their demands, Frankie would share the fiscal realities, and by the end of the spring semester, they would reach an agreement to be voted on by the faculty. The agreement would apply to all employees. At any given moment, the faculty representatives either spoke as strong advocates for staff or stated that they could not speak for staff.

During one year's deliberation, the equity of compensation models was discussed. "If we use a flat percent," Professor Mensch suggested, "it will continue to grow the gap between the highest paid and the lowest paid. A flat increase will be more equitable." The other faculty members unanimously wanted equity, and at the same time, realized that this approach would lower their raise. Provost Earnest, pointing out the mixed messages, asked if the faculty might include staff in these meetings, so that the staff could advocate for themselves. The faculty chair agreed to bring it up to the staff senate leadership, Stevie Staff, and within a year, staff were allowed to attend but not vote.

CONSIDER:

1. How is shared governance being used in this case study? Is it effective? If not, what changes might be considered?

2. What are the equity and inclusion issues highlighted by this case study? How do you imagine future deliberations proceeding?

3. What possibilities for shared governance does this structural change invite?

4. Where are some of the potential power dynamic pitfalls within this solution?

5. As you read the case study, did you have an image for each character? If so, what gender and ethnicity did you imagine? (This might help you uncover some implicit bias.)

Now consider the almost infinite possibilities of people's identities in the case study, and the shifting power dynamics:

a. Gender: If you imagined a character as either male or female, try switching your image to another gender, including non-binary.

b. Ethnicity: If you imagined a character as a particular ethnicity, try switching your image to another ethnicity.

c. Intersectional identities: Imagine different permutations of interactions between people of varying intersecting identities. (For example, imagine the case study with all White men, all White women, all African American men, all African American women, all men of color of different ethnicities, all women of color of different ethnicities, mixed genders of the same ethnicity, mixed genders across ethnicities.)

As you imagine different identities, consider the potential effects on interactions.

Would your answers or suggestions to any of the questions asked above change, given shifting power dynamics, across all of these intersecting permutations?

CASE STUDY #4: THE CASE OF THE ROVING EMPLOYEE

Frankie Fiscal has been promoted to campus CFO and VP after working in the business and finance division for several years. Frankie is thrilled to be promoted, and life is good until Frankie realizes that Drew Drama has just been transferred to the CFO's office. The outgoing CFO, who had already signed retirement papers, agreed to take Drew from another unit, where the unit head had complained bitterly about Drew's poor performance and the constant turmoil created by Drew's behavior.

Frankie is all too familiar with Drew, who has moved from one unit to another for years with no improvement in performance or temperament. A few of Drew's supervisors have tried to address Drew's performance and behavior, including a few attempts to separate Drew from the university. Each supervisor would meet with HR Director Mona Volador and leave the meeting cautiously optimistic that they might receive assistance with the situation. But eventually, after meeting with President Petry, Mona would hold a second meeting with the supervisor, stating that they had no memory of offering to support the supervisor with corrective actions or separation. Mona, who conveniently never takes notes at meetings they attend, ultimately suggests that the best course of action is to look for a "better fit" for Drew in another unit.

Frankie begins the new position on a Monday, and by Wednesday, it is clear that Drew will not work out. Frankie meets with Mona to discuss options and leaves the meeting with some hope, but Frankie's hopes are dashed during the second meeting with Mona. The only relief Mona can offer Frankie is assistance with transferring Drew to another office.

To make matters worse, Frankie learns from a colleague in the advancement division that Drew is related to Big Bucks Bentley, an alum, board member, and major donor who is in the process of establishing another multimillion-dollar endowment.

Feeling trapped, Frankie decides the only way to resolve this is to demote Drew (along with a decrease in salary), hoping that they will resign soon.

Drew loudly complains about this situation and files a grievance through the shared governance committee responsible for personnel complaints. Drew's longevity has resulted in longstanding relationships among many on campus, including many on this committee. The committee's task is to investigate and make recommendations to the appropriate VP; this process in the past has often resulted in conflict, as the recommendations are often not agreed to by any VP.

CONSIDER:

1. What potential shared governance issues do you note in this case study? Consider trust, assumptions, and process issues.

2. Personnel matters often are difficult within shared governance, due to confidentiality concerns. How might this process be affected by confidentiality? What can/should the committee members be told about the past history?

3. What do you and/or your institution believe is the role for a shared governance grievance committee for personnel matters?

4. As you read the case study, did you have an image for each character? If so, what gender and ethnicity did you imagine? (This might help you uncover some implicit bias.)

   Now consider the almost infinite possibilities of people's identities in the case study, and the shifting power dynamics:

   a. Gender: If you imagined a character as either male or female, try switching your image to another gender, including non-binary.

   b. Ethnicity: If you imagined a character as a particular ethnicity, try switching your image to another ethnicity.

   c. Intersectional identities: Imagine different permutations of interactions between people of varying intersecting identities. (For example, imagine the case study with all White men, all White women, all African American men, all African American women, all men of color of different ethnicities, all women of color of different ethnicities, mixed genders of the same ethnicity, mixed genders across ethnicities.)

   As you imagine different identities, consider the potential effects on interactions.

   Would your answers or suggestions to any of the questions asked above change, given shifting power dynamics, across all of these intersecting permutations?

CASE STUDY #5: THE CASE OF THE DECELERATED CAMPUS CENTERS

JRU, like many institutions, is working to remove a deficit from the annual budget. The administrators have made good progress over the past two years, but there is still a need for caution around where to dedicate funds for new initiatives. As part of this process, the entire institution has been involved in conversations about strategic directions. A faculty committee, elected by the faculty and reporting through the faculty senate, were excited to be invited to the quarterly Board of Trustees' meetings for one aspect of these conversations. This committee is composed of Abby Monkson, Pat Pompous, Professor Mensch, Professor Singer, Harper Hustle, Professor Combative, and Murphy Meager.

At the last meeting, excitement rose as the faculty and trustees began to discuss the possibility of campus Centers for Excellence. Monkson, a proponent of 'learning in place,' suggested a center in which the students would do service learning in the local community. "It will only take a director and an administrative staff to organize this—and think of all that the students can do for others!" The look in Monkson's eyes suggested they were already envisioning themself as director. Each added their own ideas about a center, ranging from one that would provide concerts throughout the community (Singer's suggestion), to one that would be a Center for Excellence in Firefly Research, a specialty of Hustle's.

The meeting ended with exhilaration for most. The faculty were already thinking about the creation of multiple centers, each with their own director (with course releases for all the administrative work needed), and the trustees were glad to see that the faculty were engaged rather than complaining. The only people who were not happy were the cabinet members present: President Petry, Provost Earnest, and CFO Fiscal.

At the next cabinet meeting, the creation of centers was on the agenda. Since these centers would all have an academic focus, Provost Earnest was asked to move forward on them. Earnest, well aware of the financial implications, decided to create a task force for the development of the centers. Earnest wrote a charge to the task force but did not include a timeline, and then reached out to the faculty senate to help find members for the task force. The task force was asked to:

- Use data to inform their recommendations to the provost.

- Develop guidelines and criteria for the development of centers.

- Create a guide for budget development, as well.

CONSIDER:

6. Make a list of the shared governance structures in this case study. Does their work (or potential work) meet the definition of shared governance and/or consultation?

7. Assuming good intentions, consider the various work tempos in the case study, including the discussion about centers at the BOT meeting and the lack of timeline in the charge to the task force. What (and who) does the tempo's urgency, or lack thereof, serve?

8. How would you handle this task, if you were Provost Earnest?

9. How would you approach this task, if you were on the Center Creation Task Force?

10. As you read the case study, did you have an image for each character? If so, what gender and ethnicity did you imagine? (This might help you uncover some implicit bias.)

Now consider the almost infinite possibilities of people's identities in the case study, and the shifting power dynamics:

a. Gender: If you imagined a character as either male or female, try switching your image to another gender, including non-binary.

b. Ethnicity: If you imagined a character as a particular ethnicity, try switching your image to another ethnicity.

c. Intersectional identities: Imagine different permutations of interactions between people of varying intersecting identities. (For example, imagine the case study with all White men, all White women, all African American men, all African American women, all men of color of different ethnicities, all women of color of different ethnicities, mixed genders of the same ethnicity, mixed genders across ethnicities.)

As you imagine different identities, consider the potential effects on interactions.

Would your answers or suggestions to any of the questions asked above change, given shifting power dynamics, across all of these intersecting permutations?

CASE STUDY #6: THE CASE OF THE PREMATURE PROMOTION

Provost Earnest receives a recommendation to promote a faculty member (or staff) from the review committee of their peers. As each recommendation is read, it is clear that the committee, chaired by Professor Mensch, ignored some important information that contradicts granting promotion at this time. The Provost cannot in good faith recommend promotion during this cycle. The person can submit for promotion again the following semester or year and has time to address the deficits in their performance. Provost Earnest plans to not recommend for promotion and wants to be sure that shared governance is not violated in doing so.

CONSIDER:

1. In what processes should the Provost engage?

2. To whom should Earnest speak, and how might they frame the issues?

3. As you read the case study, did you have an image for each character? If so, what gender and ethnicity did you imagine? (This might help you uncover some implicit bias.)

Now consider the almost infinite possibilities of people's identities in the case study, and the shifting power dynamics:

a. Gender: If you imagined a character as either male or female, try switching your image to another gender, including non-binary.

b. Ethnicity: If you imagined a character as a particular ethnicity, try switching your image to another ethnicity.

c. Intersectional identities: Imagine different permutations of interactions between people of varying intersecting identities. (For example, imagine the case study with all White men, all White women, all African American men, all African American women, all men of color of different ethnicities, all women of color of different ethnicities, mixed genders of the same ethnicity, mixed genders across ethnicities.)

As you imagine different identities, consider the potential effects on interactions.

Would your answers or suggestions to any of the questions asked above change, given shifting power dynamics, across all of these intersecting permutations?

CASE STUDY #7: THE CASE OF MOUNTAINS AND MOLEHILLS

President Petry and Provost Earnest are rarely invited to attend the Faculty Senate meetings, making it difficult to advance important strategic directions for the institution. The executive committee of the Senate agrees to meet with them prior to and after each Senate meeting, with the stated purpose of discussing important strategic items. However, the Faculty Senate president, Abby Monkson, always starts the meeting with a list of minor concerns raised by the faculty, which typically takes the whole meeting time. When questioned, Abby notes that these little items can get out of control very quickly, and the intent is to help solve them before they can grow. President Petry and Provost Earnest often and gently point out the purpose of the meeting, to no avail.

CONSIDER:

1. As you read this case study, how does this process fit with the purpose of effective shared governance?

2. What other communication strategies might President Petry and Provost Earnest do to advance strategic directions within this meeting? What would it take to make that even possible?

3. What data might Petry and Earnest share to help advance strategic directions?

4. How might they engage in radical transparency?

5. As you read the case study, did you have an image for each character? If so, what gender and ethnicity did you imagine? (This might help you uncover some implicit bias.)

Now consider the almost infinite possibilities of people's identities in the case study, and the shifting power dynamics:

a. Gender: If you imagined a character as either male or female, try switching your image to another gender, including non-binary.

b. Ethnicity: If you imagined a character as a particular ethnicity, try switching your image to another ethnicity.

c. Intersectional identities: Imagine different permutations of interactions between people of varying intersecting identities. (For example, imagine the case study with all White men, all White women, all African American men, all African American women, all men of color of different ethnicities, all women of color of different ethnicities, mixed genders of the same ethnicity, mixed genders across ethnicities.)

As you imagine different identities, consider the potential effects on interactions.

Would your answers or suggestions to any of the questions asked above change, given shifting power dynamics, across all of these intersecting permutations?

CASE STUDY #8: THE CASE OF BUILDING COMMUNITY BY CLASSICS

During a brief gap between named provosts, Dr. Pat Pompous was named Acting Provost. They were excited that it was their turn to lead Academic Affairs. They had lived through seven provosts during their time at JRU and all their various roles in shared governance, and they had often been a vocal critic of the decisions of administration. Now it was their turn to lead!

The first step, thought Pompous, was to build community. They promptly started sending out a newsletter to Academic Affairs each week, starting with a quote from ancient Greek and Roman philosophers, since their doctorate was in the Classics. Pompous wanted the faculty to know they were one of them, a true scholar. In fact, Pompous liked this idea so much that they started each meeting by reading a quote, and embedded classical references in reports, committee charges, and personnel documents. The Academic Affairs leadership team, including Deans Lackey and Wink, started hearing snide comments about the use of these quotes among their faculty. Privately, they discussed whether or not to communicate this reaction to Pompous.

CONSIDER:

1. Pompous was proud of their discipline. How might these quotes impact the effectiveness of their communications as an administrator?

2. Should Lackey or Wink tell Pompous about the background chatter? If so, what might be effective ways to communicate this to Pompous, with the intent to help the communication coming out of Academic Affairs to move along its strategic agenda?

3. As you read the case study, did you have an image for each character? If so, what gender and ethnicity did you imagine? (This might help you uncover some implicit bias.)

   Now consider the almost infinite possibilities of people's identities in the case study, and the shifting power dynamics:

   a. Gender: If you imagined a character as either male or female, try switching your image to another gender, including non-binary.

   b. Ethnicity: If you imagined a character as a particular ethnicity, try switching your image to another ethnicity.

   c. Intersectional identities: Imagine different permutations of interactions between people of varying intersecting identities. (For example, imagine the case study with all White men, all White women, all African American men, all African American women, all men of color of different ethnicities, all women of color of different ethnicities, mixed genders of the same ethnicity, mixed genders across ethnicities.)

   As you imagine different identities, consider the potential effects on interactions.

   Would your answers or suggestions to any of the questions asked above change, given shifting power dynamics, across all of these intersecting permutations?

Case Study #9: The Case of the Backpedaling (Or is it Backstabbing?) Tenure Appointment

Dean Wink, for three years prior to Professor Combative's tenure application, has carefully crafted responses to all personnel processes regarding them, and has meticulously noted all areas needed for improvement prior to a successful tenure bid. Combative submits their tenure portfolio, which gets mixed support from his department and receives a 5-4 vote in favor; further, they are not recommended from the shared governance Rank and Tenure committee. Dean Wink concurs that there are significant gaps in the record and does not recommend tenure to Provost Earnest, who concurs. However, President Petry decides to grant tenure; Dean Wink suspects Petry's motivation is to avoid conflict.

CONSIDER:

1. Does the shared governance process described in this case study fit with the typical process at your institution?

2. Was a shared governance process followed, and was the result congruent with why the process was designed?

3. What dynamic does this create for Dean Wink regarding future tenure recommendations? Should Dean Wink address this with anyone and, if so, what might they say or hope to accomplish?

4. What dynamic does this decision create for the department faculty and the faculty serving on the Rank and Tenure committee?

5. As you read the case study, did you have an image for each character? If so, what gender and ethnicity did you imagine? (This might help you uncover some implicit bias.)

    Now consider the almost infinite possibilities of people's identities in the case study, and the shifting power dynamics:

    a. Gender: If you imagined a character as either male or female, try switching your image to another gender, including non-binary.

    b. Ethnicity: If you imagined a character as a particular ethnicity, try switching your image to another ethnicity.

    c. Intersectional identities: Imagine different permutations of interactions between people of varying intersecting identities. (For example, imagine the case study with all White men, all White women, all African American men, all African American women, all men of color of different ethnicities, all women of color of different ethnicities, mixed genders of the same ethnicity, mixed genders across ethnicities.)

    As you imagine different identities, consider the potential effects on interactions.

    Would your answers or suggestions to any of the questions asked above change, given shifting power dynamics, across all of these intersecting permutations?

CASE STUDY #10: THE CASE OF THE DENSE DEAN

Dean Lackey was charged with overseeing the selection of a department chair, for a department that was already fractured along gender lines. The departmental bylaws require each candidate to make a presentation to the other faculty, followed by an anonymous vote for each candidate. The results of the vote are shared in the aggregate to all departmental faculty. Ultimately, Dean Lackey has to endorse the elected candidate, and a recommendation is then made to the Provost for appointment to a three-year term.

Typically, there is just one candidate. However, this year is different, and there are *two* candidates. To address this situation, Dean Lackey inserts a new requirement for the vote; after each presentation, each voting member must first vote either *acceptable* or *not acceptable* for each candidate, followed by a ranking of the acceptable candidates. Candidate One, who is male, is voted in as Chair, with unanimous 'acceptable' votes. Candidate Two, who is female, receives several 'unacceptable' votes. All votes in aggregate were shared with the entire department. Provost Earnest finds out about this process when Candidate Two tells President Petry about the results, hinting at a lawsuit.

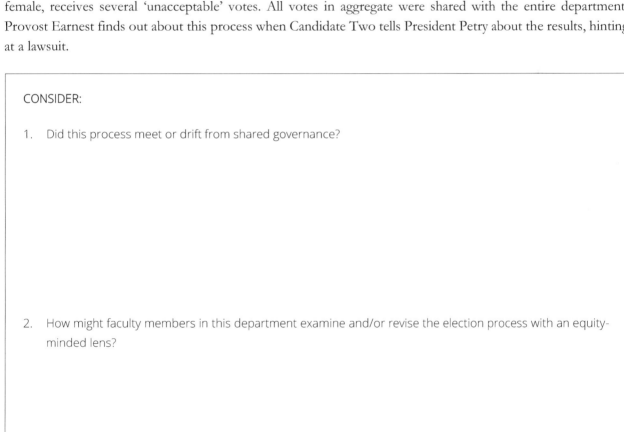

CONSIDER:

1. Did this process meet or drift from shared governance?

2. How might faculty members in this department examine and/or revise the election process with an equity-minded lens?

3. How might the surprise to both supervisor(s) and the outcome have been averted?

4. How might Provost Earnest and/or President Petry deal with this—and with whom?

5. As you read the case study, did you have an image for each character? If so, what gender and ethnicity did you imagine? (This might help you uncover some implicit bias.)

Now consider the almost infinite possibilities of people's identities in the case study, and the shifting power dynamics:

a. Gender: If you imagined a character as either male or female, try switching your image to another gender, including non-binary.

b. Ethnicity: If you imagined a character as a particular ethnicity, try switching your image to another ethnicity.

c. Intersectional identities: Imagine different permutations of interactions between people of varying intersecting identities. (For example, imagine the case study with all White men, all White women, all African American men, all African American women, all men of color of different ethnicities, all women of color of different ethnicities, mixed genders of the same ethnicity, mixed genders across ethnicities.)

As you imagine different identities, consider the potential effects on interactions.

Would your answers or suggestions to any of the questions asked above change, given shifting power dynamics, across all of these intersecting permutations?

CASE STUDY #11: THE CASE OF THE SELF-ASSURED SENATORS

In preparing for faculty and staff to return to campus in fall 2020 during the COVID-19 pandemic, the HR department works carefully with the campus health officer to follow the CDC guidelines. Included are criteria regarding employee behavior and safety protocols on campus, as well as criteria for waivers to work on campus. Led by Abby Monkson, the faculty Senate sends a resolution to President Petry, insisting that they should review and decide on each waiver submitted by faculty; Monkson makes it clear that they think most, if not all, should be granted.

CONSIDER:

1. What parts of this, if any, are a reasonable request within faculty shared governance?

2. Are there other groups/constituencies that should be involved via shared governance, in addition to or instead of the faculty?

3. What process/structure might be set up to involve a shared governance process?

4. As you read the case study, did you have an image for each character? If so, what gender and ethnicity did you imagine? (This might help you uncover some implicit bias.)

    Now consider the almost infinite possibilities of people's identities in the case study, and the shifting power dynamics:

    a. Gender: If you imagined a character as either male or female, try switching your image to another gender, including non-binary.

    b. Ethnicity: If you imagined a character as a particular ethnicity, try switching your image to another ethnicity.

    c. Intersectional identities: Imagine different permutations of interactions between people of varying intersecting identities. (For example, imagine the case study with all White men, all White women, all African American men, all African American women, all men of color of different ethnicities, all women of color of different ethnicities, mixed genders of the same ethnicity, mixed genders across ethnicities.)

    As you imagine different identities, consider the potential effects on interactions.

    Would your answers or suggestions to any of the questions asked above change, given shifting power dynamics, across all of these intersecting permutations?

CASE STUDY #12: THE CASE OF THE TIRE TRACKS ON THE BACK

It's that time of year, when Provost Earnest meets with all the deans to get their input about allocation of faculty positions. This year, due to a substantial salary increase for all faculty, there is a very limited amount left in the personnel budget, only allowing for one new position. The Provost and the deans discuss their colleges' needs and the budget situation at length, over several meetings. Each dean is able to advocate strongly for their needs, and all come to consensus about the most compelling position needed, and a position is allocated to a department in Dean Wink's college. Further, the deans discuss and strategize about how to communicate this news.

At the next chairs' council, Dean Lackey tells their chairs that Provost Earnest just refused to allocate funding for any of their positions, offering no rationale. When meeting with the chairs in their college, Dean Outsider is told that this would never have happened under Dean Perfect.

CONSIDER:

1. Was a shared governance process followed, including consultation?

2. Who is owning their responsibility and authority in this situation?

3. What are the effects when blame is shifted to someone other than the person who oversees the unit?

4. How/where are power dynamics operating in this case study?

5. As you read the case study, did you have an image for each character? If so, what gender and ethnicity did you imagine? (This might help you uncover some implicit bias.)

    Now consider the almost infinite possibilities of people's identities in the case study, and the shifting power dynamics:

    a. Gender: If you imagined a character as either male or female, try switching your image to another gender, including non-binary.

    b. Ethnicity: If you imagined a character as a particular ethnicity, try switching your image to another ethnicity.

    c. Intersectional identities: Imagine different permutations of interactions between people of varying intersecting identities. (For example, imagine the case study with all White men, all White women, all African American men, all African American women, all men of color of different ethnicities, all women of color of different ethnicities, mixed genders of the same ethnicity, mixed genders across ethnicities.)

    As you imagine different identities, consider the potential effects on interactions.

    Would your answers or suggestions to any of the questions asked above change, given shifting power dynamics, across all of these intersecting permutations?

CASE STUDY #13: THE CASE OF MUTINY IN THE MUSIC DEPARTMENT

The university's fall 2022 first-year class was down 7% from fall 2021, and returning students are down 5%. Under ordinary circumstances, the university can make up for any small downturns in fall enrollment the following spring by drawing on a large pool of community college transfers, but that will not happen this year. To make matters worse, fall 2023 enrollment projections do not look good. Provost Earnest and the deans are aware that they must begin planning for budget cuts and resource reallocation plans. The Provost schedules a meeting with Abby Monkson, faculty senate President, to clarify a consultation process.

Professor Singer, Chair of the music department, is usually an advocate for using elected bodies to voice the faculty perspective. But in a lengthy email addressed to Provost Earnest and the Dean, Professor Singer expresses distrust of even the music department's elected senators to properly represent the department in a senate full of people from larger departments with higher-demand programs. The email states that the stakes are too high to trust the faculty senate to advocate successfully for a very small and often overlooked department, and that in times of economic downturn, the arts always seem to be the first thing to go. Therefore, states the professor, they will form their own separate consultation group that will meet with the Provost and Dean and that any feedback about the music department from the faculty senate should be disregarded.

The chairs of several small departments get wind of the mutiny in the music department and decide that they, too, will form their own independent groups.

CONSIDER:

1. Consider the shared governance process described above. What might be working well, and where are there areas for improvement?

2. How should Provost Earnest respond to Professor Singer and the other mutinous department chairs?

3. As you read the case study, did you have an image for each character? If so, what gender and ethnicity did you imagine? (This might help you uncover some implicit bias.)

Now consider the almost infinite possibilities of people's identities in the case study, and the shifting power dynamics:

a. Gender: If you imagined a character as either male or female, try switching your image to another gender, including non-binary.

b. Ethnicity: If you imagined a character as a particular ethnicity, try switching your image to another ethnicity.

c. Intersectional identities: Imagine different permutations of interactions between people of varying intersecting identities. (For example, imagine the case study with all White men, all White women, all African American men, all African American women, all men of color of different ethnicities, all women of color of different ethnicities, mixed genders of the same ethnicity, mixed genders across ethnicities.)

As you imagine different identities, consider the potential effects on interactions.

Would your answers or suggestions to any of the questions asked above change, given shifting power dynamics, across all of these intersecting permutations?

CASE STUDY #14: THE CASE OF THE PREFERENTIAL PERSONNEL PROCESS

President Petry is concerned that when alumni apply for jobs on campus, few, if any, are hired. The President submits a policy revision to the policy committee, which asks them to consider adding preferential language to the personnel process. The policy language would provide alumni job candidates with automatic consideration as finalists for any positions for which they are qualified. It does not mandate that they are hired, only that, if qualified, they are able to be among the finalists in the interview process. The President runs this first by the faculty senate President, Abby Monkson, and they support it. However, when vetted in the policy committee and the full faculty senate, the new language is defeated for recommendation forward.

CONSIDER:

1. Consider the shared governance process described above. What is working well and what might be improved?

2. What are the politics involved in this situation, from the perspectives of alumni, advancement, faculty, staff, board of trustees?

3. Was this a reasonable policy change request by the President?

4. Were there any other processes needed to increase the likelihood of the policy being recommended?

5. As you read the case study, did you have an image for each character? If so, what gender and ethnicity did you imagine? (This might help you uncover some implicit bias.)

Now consider the almost infinite possibilities of people's identities in the case study, and the shifting power dynamics:

a. Gender: If you imagined a character as either male or female, try switching your image to another gender, including non-binary.

b. Ethnicity: If you imagined a character as a particular ethnicity, try switching your image to another ethnicity.

c. Intersectional identities: Imagine different permutations of interactions between people of varying intersecting identities. (For example, imagine the case study with all White men, all White women, all African American men, all African American women, all men of color of different ethnicities, all women of color of different ethnicities, mixed genders of the same ethnicity, mixed genders across ethnicities.)

As you imagine different identities, consider the potential effects on interactions.

Would your answers or suggestions to any of the questions asked above change, given shifting power dynamics, across all of these intersecting permutations?

~

CASE STUDY #15: THE CASE OF THE SECRET SURVEY

Dr. Dissatisfied thinks that there is no "real" shared governance in the division of academic affairs and that Abby Monkson, faculty senate President, along with the Provost and all the deans, must be removed. Dr. Dissatisfied and two of the 50 faculty senators meet with Abby and say that they will call for a vote of no confidence on Abby at the next faculty senate meeting. Shaken, Abby inquires about and listens to their concerns and promises to do what it takes to give Dr. Dissatisfied and the two faculty senators more decision-making power in academic affairs.

They all meet again the next day, and Dr. Dissatisfied strongly recommends that Abby, as faculty senate President, emails a survey to all faculty members rating the Provost and each dean on adherence to "real" shared governance. Dr. Dissatisfied tells Abby that they have already developed the survey using a free survey tool found on the internet; therefore, the survey can go out using the faculty senate email account before the end of the day.

The next morning, the campus is abuzz with talk of the survey. The 48 faculty senators who did not know about or attend Dr. Dissatisfied's meetings with Abby are angry that a survey was launched without their knowledge or consent. The Chair of computer science comments that the free survey tool that was used does not adhere to university data security and confidentiality protocols. Someone forwards the survey to several students, and the students create a game to see how many times they can open and answer the survey before they are shut out.

Undaunted by the comments heard about the botched implementation, Dr. Dissatisfied and a reluctant Abby insist on meeting with Provost Earnest and the deans to discuss the survey results and make their demands.

CONSIDER:

1. Consider the shared governance process described above. What is working well and what might be improved?

---

2. Should Provost Earnest take the meeting? If so, what are the implications for shared governance, and how should the Provost approach the meeting? If not, what should the Provost communicate to Dr. Dissatisfied, Abby, and the division, and *how* should the Provost communicate it?

3. What are the politics involved in this situation, from the perspectives of faculty and administrators?

4. As you read the case study, did you have an image for each character? If so, what gender and ethnicity did you imagine? (This might help you uncover some implicit bias.)

    Now consider the almost infinite possibilities of people's identities in the case study, and the shifting power dynamics:

    a. Gender: If you imagined a character as either male or female, try switching your image to another gender, including non-binary.

    b. Ethnicity: If you imagined a character as a particular ethnicity, try switching your image to another ethnicity.

    c. Intersectional identities: Imagine different permutations of interactions between people of varying intersecting identities. (For example, imagine the case study with all White men, all White women, all African American men, all African American women, all men of color of different ethnicities, all women of color of different ethnicities, mixed genders of the same ethnicity, mixed genders across ethnicities.)

    As you imagine different identities, consider the potential effects on interactions.

    Would your answers or suggestions to any of the questions asked above change, given shifting power dynamics, across all of these intersecting permutations?

CASE STUDY #16: THE CASE OF THE DEFEATED DEPARTMENT—PART A

The Cultural Studies department members were delighted to be awarded a tenure-track position, which would bring their faculty cohort to four full-time faculty. After a national search, the search and screen committee members are pleased to present their candidate of choice to Dean Wink. Out of four finalists, they recommend an internal candidate, Murphy Meager, to Dean Wink. The committee notes that although they didn't agree with this recommendation, the department vote as a whole (which included all full- and part-time faculty) chose Meager, who was currently serving as an adjunct in the department.

Dean Wink had met all the candidates and thought Meager was not qualified; the Dean would have ranked them fourth. Further, Dean Wink is curious about the representation from the search committee that they don't think Meager is the best, but that the full department does. Dean Wink holds the final authority about who is hired.

CONSIDER:

1. Consider the shared governance process described in the case study. What worked well and what could be improved?

2. To reach a decision, what information does Dean Wink need, and from whom?

3. If Dean Wink decides to not offer the position to Meager, what communication is needed and to whom?

4. What potential pitfalls does Dean Wink need to be prepared to address/manage?

5. As you read the case study, did you have an image for each character? If so, what gender and ethnicity did you imagine? (This might help you uncover some implicit bias.)

   Now consider the almost infinite possibilities of people's identities in the case study, and the shifting power dynamics:

   a. Gender: If you imagined a character as either male or female, try switching your image to another gender, including non-binary.

   b. Ethnicity: If you imagined a character as a particular ethnicity, try switching your image to another ethnicity.

   c. Intersectional identities: Imagine different permutations of interactions between people of varying intersecting identities. (For example, imagine the case study with all White men, all White women, all African American men, all African American women, all men of color of different ethnicities, all women of color of different ethnicities, mixed genders of the same ethnicity, mixed genders across ethnicities.)

   As you imagine different identities, consider the potential effects on interactions.

   Would your answers or suggestions to any of the questions asked above change, given shifting power dynamics, across all of these intersecting permutations?

CASE STUDY #17: THE CASE OF THE DEFEATED DEPARTMENT—PART B

Dean Wink met with the entire department, who provided no further evidence of how Meager might rank over the other three candidates, or even be qualified. Wink was able to get the department to rank the other three, and Wink let them know they would be offering the position to the next candidate in line.

The department responds by mounting a campaign to hire Meager, involving students who show up at a faculty senate meeting exclaiming, "We know that Meager might not be qualified, but we want them hired anyway." Dean Wink does not consider Meager to be qualified and plans to offer the position to one of the other three, using the ranking begrudgingly provided by the department.

CONSIDER:

1. What parts of this case study involve shared governance, and which parts involve personnel matters outside the purview of shared governance?

2. What can Dean Wink do or say to the students or faculty colleagues, within the ethics of best hiring practices?

---

3.   Is there anything that HR director Mona Volador might need to do about the department faculty's behaviors?

4.   What concerns might Dean Wink have about the new hire and their entry into the department, and how might the Dean deal with those?

5. As you read the case study, did you have an image for each character? If so, what gender and ethnicity did you imagine? (This might help you uncover some implicit bias.)

Now consider the almost infinite possibilities of people's identities in the case study, and the shifting power dynamics:

a. Gender: If you imagined a character as either male or female, try switching your image to another gender, including non-binary.

b. Ethnicity: If you imagined a character as a particular ethnicity, try switching your image to another ethnicity.

c. Intersectional identities: Imagine different permutations of interactions between people of varying intersecting identities. (For example, imagine the case study with all White men, all White women, all African American men, all African American women, all men of color of different ethnicities, all women of color of different ethnicities, mixed genders of the same ethnicity, mixed genders across ethnicities.)

As you imagine different identities, consider the potential effects on interactions.

Would your answers or suggestions to any of the questions asked above change, given shifting power dynamics, across all of these intersecting permutations?

CASE STUDY #18: THE CASE OF THE ACCREDITATION AMBUSH

The university is engaged in its decennial regional reaccreditation process, and things appear to be going swimmingly. A fifty-person self-study team consisting of faculty, staff, students, and administrators is working together to develop a comprehensive self-study document addressing the 12 accreditation standards with accompanying institutional data. Pleased with the high level of cooperation and the high quality of the self-study report, President Petry sends a campus-wide email a week before the site visit to thank everyone for their hard work and cooperation, and to share that the pre-visit feedback from the evaluation team is extremely positive.

Dr. Dogma refused to serve on the campus self-study team, to reinforce his stance opposing assessment of student learning using anything other than class grades. Dr. Dogma considers himself the 'moral compass' of the campus and believes that he is the only thing standing between the university and a downward slide into an ethical abyss. President Petry's email provokes his ire. He feels compelled to balance the self-study team's report with his own state-of-the-university report—a document with no mention of the 12 accreditation standards and that is wholly lacking in official institutional data.

Unbeknownst to President Petry, Dr. Dogma emails the evaluation team Chair to request a private meeting during the site visit. The evaluation team Chair writes back agreeing to the meeting, and Dr. Dogma invites a few like-minded faculty members to join him. The evaluation team Chair notifies the President that she has agreed to a meeting with Dr. Dogma. The President calls an emergency cabinet meeting to get advice on the best course of action given that Dr. Dogma has been granted a meeting with the evaluation team Chair. Provost Earnest receives a clandestinely obtained copy of Dr. Dogma's document from a faculty member who worked on the self-study team. The Provost makes copies and takes them to the cabinet meeting.

CONSIDER:

1. What aspects, if any, of this case study involve shared governance?

2. How should President Petry handle the situation in the context of shared governance?

3. As you read the case study, did you have an image for each character? If so, what gender and ethnicity did you imagine? (This might help you uncover some implicit bias.)

Now consider the almost infinite possibilities of people's identities in the case study, and the shifting power dynamics:

a. Gender: If you imagined a character as either male or female, try switching your image to another gender, including non-binary.

b. Ethnicity: If you imagined a character as a particular ethnicity, try switching your image to another ethnicity.

c. Intersectional identities: Imagine different permutations of interactions between people of varying intersecting identities. (For example, imagine the case study with all White men, all White women, all African American men, all African American women, all men of color of different ethnicities, all women of color of different ethnicities, mixed genders of the same ethnicity, mixed genders across ethnicities.)

As you imagine different identities, consider the potential effects on interactions.

Would your answers or suggestions to any of the questions asked above change, given shifting power dynamics, across all of these intersecting permutations?

CASE STUDY #19: THE CASE OF THE PENSIVE PRESIDENT

President Petry is in a pensive mood and is reviewing the list of goals developed in year one. Feeling tired and overwhelmed—especially since the advent of the pandemic and the concomitant enrollment downturn—the President decides to finally tackle those goals that never made it to the first-year to-do list. Given the state of the world, and with two years remaining on a five-year contract, the President wants to spend the remaining time focused on accomplishing at least three of these goals. Before Petry can figure out which goals might be possible, they first consider the shared governance processes, if needed, for each.

First, note which of these goals might require a shared governance process. If shared governance and/or consultation is needed, suggest what groups and/or processes Petry would need to engage to accomplish each of them:

GOALS	SHARED GOVERNANCE/ CONSULTATION NEEDED? (Y/N)	WHAT GROUPS AND/OR PROCESSES DOES PETRY NEED TO ENGAGE?
Establish a center for faculty development		
Conduct fundraising campaign for an alumni walk of fame		
Reduce deferred maintenance by 10%		
Break ground on a new performing arts building		
Rebrand the institution, including a redesigned logo and new slogan		

Goals	Shared governance/ consultation needed? (y/n)	What groups and/or processes does Petry need to engage?
Become a test-optional or test-blind campus		
Establish a research foundation		
Expand athletics program		
Restructure academic affairs		
Establish a center for equity and inclusion		

CONSIDER:

1. As you read the case study, did you have an image for President Petry? If so, what gender and ethnicity did you imagine? (This might help you uncover some implicit bias.)

    Now consider the almost infinite possibilities of Petry's identities in the case study, and the shifting power dynamics. How would each of the below impact how Petry's decisions might be viewed?

    a. Gender: If you imagined Petry as either male or female, try switching your image to another gender, including non-binary.

    b. Ethnicity: If you imagined Petry as a particular ethnicity, try switching your image to another ethnicity.

    c. Intersectional identities: Imagine different permutations of interactions between people of varying intersecting identities. (For example, imagine the case study with all White men, all White women, all African American men, all African American women, all men of color of different ethnicities, all women of color of different ethnicities, mixed genders of the same ethnicity, mixed genders across ethnicities.)

    As you imagine different identities, consider the potential effects on interactions.

    Would your answers or suggestions to any of the questions asked above change, given shifting power dynamics, across all of these intersecting permutations?

CASE STUDY #20: THE CASE OF THE PROVOST'S PACING PROBLEMS

Provost Earnest was pleased as they reviewed the year's initiatives, especially because everything was going according to plan with the development of new curricula for several departments. Associate Provost Tanner True had shepherded the process on behalf of Academic Affairs for the past year. The faculty in each department—including Dr. Dogma, Professor Passionate, Dr. Hopewell, Professor Singer, and Dr. Dissatisfied—were actively involved in either updating curricula or developing new programs. Deans Wink and Lackey had reviewed and approved the curricula, with only minor suggestions, which were agreed to by the respective departmental faculty. The curricula had just been vetted and approved by the university curriculum committees, both undergraduate and graduate. All that was left was for the faculty senate to vet and endorse.

In the early April meeting of the Academic Council, consisting of the deans, Assistant Provost True, Rowan Registrar, and Abby Monkson (the President of the faculty senate), Earnest realized that time was running out on this process for this academic year, then:

- Monkson reminded the group that the last faculty senate meeting was held in April, and that they needed at least two meetings to vet important proposals, such as curricula revisions.

- Monkson further reminded everyone that it was possible that the deliberations might go into the next spring, since the changes involved not just the relevant departments, but they also had effects on many majors being offered. Therefore, the earliest implementation of the changes would have to wait until the following fall.

- Rowan Registrar mentioned that once changes of this magnitude were approved, their office staff would have months of work to update the curriculum changes into the degree tracking and planning software, and asked if they could attend the faculty senate meetings to remind the senators of this important aspect of the timing. Abby said they would have to check with the Executive Committee about inviting Rowan as a guest, just this once.

Earnest wondered if there was any way to salvage the ambitious timeline to get these new programs and curricula in place before the fall. The Board of Trustees, the final approval, was meeting in June, and they were expecting some new ways to attract students. When Earnest asked the group for ideas about how to get this resolved this summer, the provost was met with silence. The meeting ended without resolution. Rowan, fuming as they left, told Earnest they needed another staff full-time to do the programming, and that they were tired of being treated poorly by faculty.

CONSIDER:

1. How did the pace and timing of the shared governance process impact this undertaking?

2. What is the role of the faculty senate, given that the curriculum committees are both shared governance bodies?

3. What is the impact of having a separate faculty senate that does not include staff on this process—and possibly on the relationships between the Registrar's office and faculty?

4. Is there any way for Earnest to speed up the process, and salvage the possibility of a fall implementation, within shared governance?

5. What resources might be needed to finish the process for a fall implementation? Consider the registrar's request and faculty contracts ending in May.

6. As you read the case study, did you have an image for each character? If so, what gender and ethnicity did you imagine? (This might help you uncover some implicit bias.)

    Now consider the almost infinite possibilities of people's identities in the case study, and the shifting power dynamics:

    a. Gender: If you imagined a character as either male or female, try switching your image to another gender, including non-binary.

    b. Ethnicity: If you imagined a character as a particular ethnicity, try switching your image to another ethnicity.

    c. Intersectional identities: Imagine different permutations of interactions between people of varying intersecting identities. (For example, imagine the case study with all White men, all White women, all African American men, all African American women, all men of color of different ethnicities, all women of color of different ethnicities, mixed genders of the same ethnicity, mixed genders across ethnicities.)

    As you imagine different identities, consider the potential effects on interactions.

    Would your answers or suggestions to any of the questions asked above change, given shifting power dynamics, across all of these intersecting permutations?

CASE STUDY #21: THE CASE OF THE PRIORITIZATION OF OTHERS' PROGRAMS

Like many institutions of higher education, JRU is deep in a revenue shortfall. Three years in, they have made decisions that helped to pay the bills in the short term. Frankie Fiscal got everyone's attention at the last Cabinet meeting when they provided projections for the upcoming two years. The looming enrollment cliff is only two years away, and enrollment for this year followed the trend of a 5% decline from the previous year and the year before that. Attracting students into new programs has been moderately successful, but has only brought in revenue to break even, rather than the robust enrollments predicted by the department faculty and the dean.

On the expense side of the ledger, no one has received a raise in five years. Morale is low; people are leaving. Positions may or may not have been filled based on the advocacy of the hiring manager or the finances at that moment, resulting in haphazard and non-strategic vacancies in both academic and other functions. As if this pressure is not enough, JRU is also scheduled for institutional-level accreditation next year. If the revenue and expenses are not balanced, and soon, JRU may lose accreditation and close its doors within the decade.

President Petry knows that it's time to engage in a program prioritization process. The last one, whose formal name is long forgotten but which is referred to in the campus lore as the *Prioritization of others' Programs* (PooP), did not result in any program or unit closures. Instead, it created hard feelings and damaged relationships, and that damage persists to this day.

Pettry knows that shared governance is key to the success of this process. They bring together the leadership of the institution to help plan the process, including Provost Earnest, Newby Nelson, Frankie Fiscal, Deans Wink and Lackey, Sloan Solo, Sydney Spokesperson, Coach Southpaw Sanders, the Chair of the Staff Senate, Drew Drama, Findley Fireball (President of the student senate) and the faculty senate executive committee, composed of Abby Monkson, Professor Passionate, Professor Mensch, Dr. Dissatisfied, Dr. Waverly Rockefeller Warbucks, Dr. Dogma, and Dr. Hopewell. Big Bucks Bentley was appointed as liaison to this group by the Board of Trustees.

(As you consider this case study, refer back as needed to the organizational chart for shared governance at JRU, on page 98.)

CONSIDER:

1. How might Petry manage the pressures of fiscal urgency with the need for effective shared governance processes?

    a) Weigh the pros and cons of Petry presenting this group with a plan, or working with them to develop one.

    (b) Consider who Petry might appoint as leaders of this process. How might Petry assure that constituencies are represented, and for which tasks?

    (c) Consider the timeframe of the work to be done.

(d) Consider the various tasks and match them to shared governance structures. Where might Petry use existing structures, and where might they need to create a task force or working committee? (See the organizational chart for shared governance at JRU on page 98.)

(e) Consider who has decision-making authority and the role of consultation in this situation. How should Petry design the 'flow' of activity, from deliberations to recommendations to decisions?

(f) If you were helping Petry to write the charge, what would need to be included? (See the Appendix for guidelines to writing the charge.)

2. What data will be needed to help this process? To whom should it be shared in the context of radical transparency?

3. How can Petry assure that an equity-minded lens is present during this process?

4. As you read the case study, did you have an image for each character? If so, what gender and ethnicity did you imagine? (This might help you uncover some implicit bias.)

Now consider the almost infinite possibilities of people's identities in the case study, and the shifting power dynamics:

a. Gender: If you imagined a character as either male or female, try switching your image to another gender, including non-binary.

b. Ethnicity: If you imagined a character as a particular ethnicity, try switching your image to another ethnicity.

c. Intersectional identities: Imagine different permutations of interactions between people of varying intersecting identities. (For example, imagine the case study with all White men, all White women, all African American men, all African American women, all men of color of different ethnicities, all women of color of different ethnicities, mixed genders of the same ethnicity, mixed genders across ethnicities.)

As you imagine different identities, consider the potential effects on interactions.

Would your answers or suggestions to any of the questions asked above change, given shifting power dynamics, across all of these intersecting permutations?

CASE STUDIES

APPENDIX:
WRITING AN EFFECTIVE CHARGE

ACTIVITY

Use this activity—set in our fictional Jackson Rockgrove University—to practice writing an effective charge to guide contribution from a committee, task force, or working group. Included with the activity is a template for writing a charge.

JRU is facing a budget deficit next year but isn't sure just how much. President Petry is considering an across-the-board cut, but Provost Earnest knows that an across-the-board cut can hurt the institution. The Provost delegates to you to figure out a more strategic approach.

You decide, in the spirit of shared governance, and recognizing the importance of transparency, to form a university-wide task force to develop a recommendation-making process to help identify which units should receive 20%, 10%, or 5% deductions. The recommendation process should involve input from all constituencies.

Write a sample task force charge using the template provided on the next page.

TEMPLATE FOR WRITING A CHARGE	
Tip: Write with clarity and parsimony.	
Context	Provide the background context as to the purpose and importance of the work to be done. Answer these questions: *Why do this work?* And, *Why now?*
Composition of the Task Force	How many are to serve? From what areas of the institution? How are they to be selected/elected? To whom do they report? Who is the chair/facilitator? (Or are you asking them to select a chair among themselves?)
Deliverable(s)	What question(s) are they to answer, and how are their answers to be provided (e.g., in a report of no more than *X* number of pages—keep it brief; or perhaps in a presentation)?
Data	Include the expectation for the use of data, and what kind of data (e.g., literature review, quantitative/descriptive data?). Include information about where to find data. What are they expected to gather themselves? Who will provide them with data, and what type? If possible, provide preliminary data with the charge.
Timeline	If possible, include a suggested timeline for tasks. *Always* include a deadline for completion.

ABOUT THE AUTHORS

SUSAN C. TURELL, PH.D.

Former Provost, Marywood University

In higher education for over 30 years, Susan brings a passion to her work for supporting people and for designing and implementing effective processes. She served in leadership as a department chair, associate provost, dean, and provost. She brings those experiences, as well as her training and practice as a psychologist, to synthesize best practices and approaches in a new paradigm about what it means to be an effective leader in 21st-century higher education. A seasoned administrator who is a teacher at heart, Susan welcomes the opportunity to share her learnings with new and aspiring leaders to strengthen their leadership skills, encourage their optimism, and support their vision for new possibilities. Susan earned her Ph.D. and M.Ed. in Counseling Psychology from the University of Houston, and her B.A. in Plan II (Honors Program) from the University of Texas-Austin. She has worked at regional comprehensive universities in both large- and small-state systems, as well as at a private religious university.

MARIA THOMPSON, PH.D.

President and CEO, Retired, Coppin State University

Maria is a career educator whose work experience spans a variety of institutional categories, including research universities, comprehensive universities, land-grant universities, urban-located, rural-located HBCUs, and PWIs. She was President and CEO of Coppin State University (CSU), Provost and Vice President for Academic Affairs at the State University of New York (SUNY), and Vice President for Research and Sponsored Programs at Tennessee State University. Maria earned her Bachelor of Science degree from Tennessee State University, a Master of Science degree from the Ohio State University, and a doctorate from the University of Tennessee, Knoxville.

Made in the USA
Columbia, SC
23 September 2024

42815720R00096